# ALL ABOUT

# Computers

# ALL ABOUT
# Computers

## Jean Atelsek

Illustrated by
## Debra Murov

Ziff-Davis Press
Emeryville, California

| | |
|---|---|
| Senior Development Editor | Melinda E. Levine |
| Copy Editor | Noelle Graney |
| Technical Reviewer | John Taschek |
| Project Coordinator | Sheila McGill |
| Proofreader | Cort Day |
| Cover Designer | Carrie English |
| Book Designer | Lory Poulson |
| Graphics Editors | Dan Brodnitz, Adrian Severynen, and Tony Jonick |
| Illustrator | Debra Murov |
| Senior Layout Artist | Bruce Lundquist |
| Layout Assistance | Debra Murov and Tony Jonick |
| Digital Prepress Specialist | Joe Schneider |
| Word Processors | Howard Blechman, Cat Haglund, and Allison Levin |
| Indexer | Mark Kmetzko |

Ziff-Davis Press books are produced on a Macintosh computer system with the following applications: FrameMaker®, Microsoft® Word, QuarkXPress®, Adobe Illustrator®, Adobe Photoshop®, Adobe Streamline™, MacLink®*Plus*, Aldus® FreeHand™, Collage Plus™.

Ziff-Davis Press
5903 Christie Avenue
Emeryville, CA 94608

ISBN 1-56276-166-8

Manufactured in the United States of America

10 9 8 7 6 5 4 3 2 1

**To my mother**

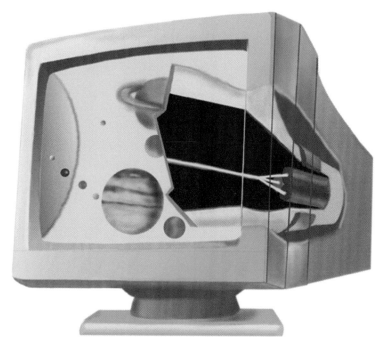

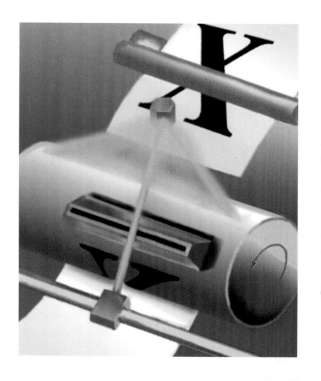

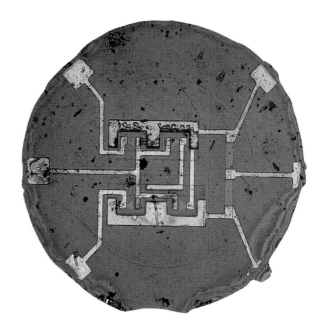

I owe many thanks to the fine staff at Ziff-Davis Press, especially to Cindy Hudson for her enthusiasm as she shaped the book's concept and guided it toward the final deadline; to Melinda Levine and Noelle Graney for their thoughtful editing; to Genevieve Ostergard for her exhaustive photo research; and to Bruce Lundquist for his patient execution of the layouts. Also, my sincere appreciation to illustrator Debra Murov and technical reviewer John Taschek for work well done. Finally, special thanks to Mike Edelhart for his contributions to and comments on the manuscript and his unfailing support throughout this project.

# What Is a Computer?

A computer is a machine that can store and process information. Computers have existed for many years because people have always needed help keeping track of information and solving problems.

Early computers were quite simple, and so were the problems they solved. Modern computers are very complicated, and the problems they solve are complex. Through the ages, information has been stored in many ways: from the pebbles or rope knots that the ancients used for counting to the microscopic electronic signals of today's powerful machines. Computers have processed information in many ways. Early processing was as slow and simple as counting stones or tying and untying knots. Modern computers process information using electronic impulses—pinpoint concentrations of energy that move at nearly the speed of light. This allows today's computers to work with amazing speed to solve a variety of difficult problems.

## THE HAND-HELD COMPUTER

These small devices are a cross between a digital watch, an electronic phone book, a calculator, and a regular personal computer. Many people use these machines for keeping track of appointments and phone numbers. They can also be used for writing documents and calculating math, and some have games, too. In hand-held computers, the software is stored permanently inside the machine. Hand-held computers weigh less than one pound each—about as much as a paperback book—so they're easy to carry around in a pocket.

## SPECIAL-USE COMPUTERS

Most modern computers can be used for a variety of tasks, depending on the software they're running. But some computers today, such as the ones in the cockpit of a Boeing 767 airplane, are like early computers because they can only run one kind of software and solve one set of problems. However, modern special-use computers do their tasks very accurately and quickly. This is valuable for important, difficult-to-solve problems. Flying passenger planes safely is just such a problem, so special computers have been developed to help fly planes. These cockpit computers use video-game-like graphics to help the pilots control the engines, keep track of the plane's location, and detect any dangers.

## THE GAME MACHINE

Game machines are special computers that work by sending images to the screen and responding to the buttons you press. Like all modern computers, they rely on two components: The computer's physical parts are called *hardware*; the set of rules a computer uses to solve a problem (or play a game) is called *software*. Working together, this computer's hardware and software challenge you as you move from one game level to the next.

The software for this game is stored in a cartridge. Some computers use disks or CDs (compact discs) to hold software, and others hold all the software on a fingernail-sized chip inside the machine. Without software, the hardware cannot solve problems; without hardware, the software cannot operate.

## THE PERSONAL COMPUTER

Depending on the software it's running, a personal computer can help write a report, solve a math problem, draw a cartoon, or play a game. You may know people who use this kind of computer at work, or you may have one at home. Personal computers were first developed in the 1970s, when the hardware components needed to store and process information became small enough to fit on a desk, and the software for solving common problems became easy enough for most people to use. Everyone loves to solve problems, so before long, millions of personal computers were in offices and homes around the world.

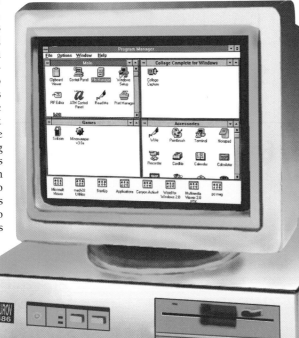

## THE SUPERCOMPUTER

Supercomputers are the most powerful computers you can find—each has the power of thousands of ordinary computers. A supercomputer's power is often measured in billions of floating-point operations per second (gigaflops), a figure that tells how quickly it can carry out mathematical calculations. The Cray C916 computer shown here is rated at 16 gigaflops. The C916 is used to solve big problems, like forecasting the weather and predicting how cars will behave in crashes. So many electronic pulses go through a supercomputer so fast that it needs a special cooling unit to keep it from overheating. The price? About $30 million.

# Where Did Computers Come From?

The development of the computer started with the need to keep track of numbers. Even before numerals were invented, people needed a way to count votes, so they placed pebbles in a bucket marked with the name of their favorite candidate. And without calculators or cash registers, how could a merchant determine how much money a customer owed? The abacus, a primitive computer, was the answer.

As math became more complex, the tools for solving math problems became more difficult to use. In the early 1800s, mathematicians had to refer to tables in huge books as they worked through their solutions. It was at the beginning of the machine age that the idea of an automatic calculating device came about. At first these devices were mechanical, but as electronics developed, so did computers.

The first electronic computer, built in the 1940s, could solve only one kind of problem: math problems. However, the more problems a computer could solve, the more valuable it became. The development of the *microprocessor*— the brains of the computer on a tiny chip—made it possible for one machine to tackle any kind of problem that people could think up rules for solving.

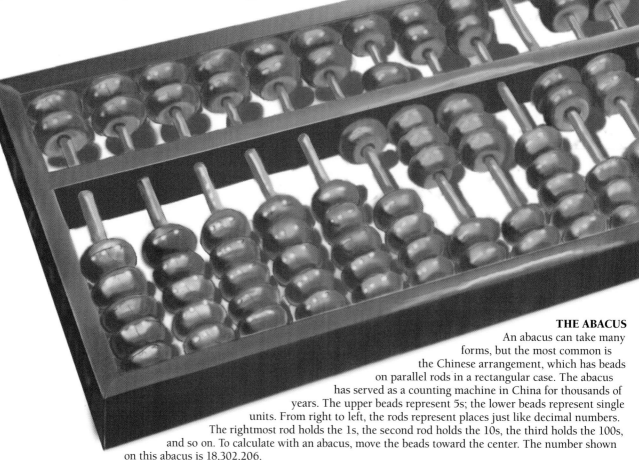

**THE ABACUS**
An abacus can take many forms, but the most common is the Chinese arrangement, which has beads on parallel rods in a rectangular case. The abacus has served as a counting machine in China for thousands of years. The upper beads represent 5s; the lower beads represent single units. From right to left, the rods represent places just like decimal numbers. The rightmost rod holds the 1s, the second rod holds the 10s, the third holds the 100s, and so on. To calculate with an abacus, move the beads toward the center. The number shown on this abacus is 18,302,206.

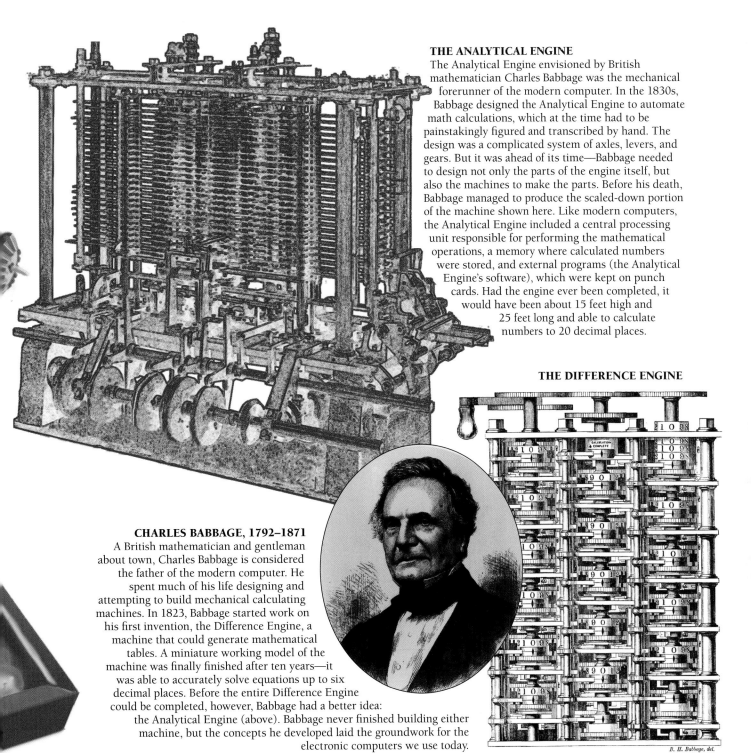

## THE ANALYTICAL ENGINE

The Analytical Engine envisioned by British mathematician Charles Babbage was the mechanical forerunner of the modern computer. In the 1830s, Babbage designed the Analytical Engine to automate math calculations, which at the time had to be painstakingly figured and transcribed by hand. The design was a complicated system of axles, levers, and gears. But it was ahead of its time—Babbage needed to design not only the parts of the engine itself, but also the machines to make the parts. Before his death, Babbage managed to produce the scaled-down portion of the machine shown here. Like modern computers, the Analytical Engine included a central processing unit responsible for performing the mathematical operations, a memory where calculated numbers were stored, and external programs (the Analytical Engine's software), which were kept on punch cards. Had the engine ever been completed, it would have been about 15 feet high and 25 feet long and able to calculate numbers to 20 decimal places.

## THE DIFFERENCE ENGINE

B. H. Babbage, del.

## CHARLES BABBAGE, 1792–1871

A British mathematician and gentleman about town, Charles Babbage is considered the father of the modern computer. He spent much of his life designing and attempting to build mechanical calculating machines. In 1823, Babbage started work on his first invention, the Difference Engine, a machine that could generate mathematical tables. A miniature working model of the machine was finally finished after ten years—it was able to accurately solve equations up to six decimal places. Before the entire Difference Engine could be completed, however, Babbage had a better idea: the Analytical Engine (above). Babbage never finished building either machine, but the concepts he developed laid the groundwork for the electronic computers we use today.

## A PREHISTORIC COMPUTER

Stonehenge, a circle of huge stones in Salisbury, England, was first built more than four thousand years ago. Some people think of it as a prehistoric computer for calculating the time of year. Stonehenge resembles a giant sundial: The shadows cast by the stones make it possible to tell what season it is. Stonehenge has proven remarkably accurate. Even now, it casts its shadow right on target as the sun rises on the first day of summer.

CONTINUED ON NEXT PAGE ➡

**COMPUTER ON A CHIP**

In 1970, Intel engineer Ted Hoff developed the first microprocessor, the 4004, to handle the computations for a line of calculators to be built by a Japanese company. The company provided specifications that would require a new set of chips for each calculator model. Hoff realized that this would be costly, so he came up with the idea of a general-purpose integrated circuit that could be programmed differently depending on the functions it had to perform. And the microprocessor was born.

A microprocessor combines all the components of a computer's central processing unit, or CPU, on a single programmable chip. When the Japanese company asked Intel to cut its prices for the chips, Intel won, in exchange, the right to sell the 4004 to other customers. At the time, Intel didn't realize the tremendous impact these chips would have. Still, the company took a chance and offered the 4004 for sale to the public in 1971. By itself, the 4004 wasn't very powerful—it had 2,250 transistors and could perform 60,000 operations per second, enough for a calculator or cash register but not adequate to power a personal computer. Still, the invention of the micro-processor made it possible to design and manufacture chips in quantity, and, ultimately, this invention launched the personal computer industry.

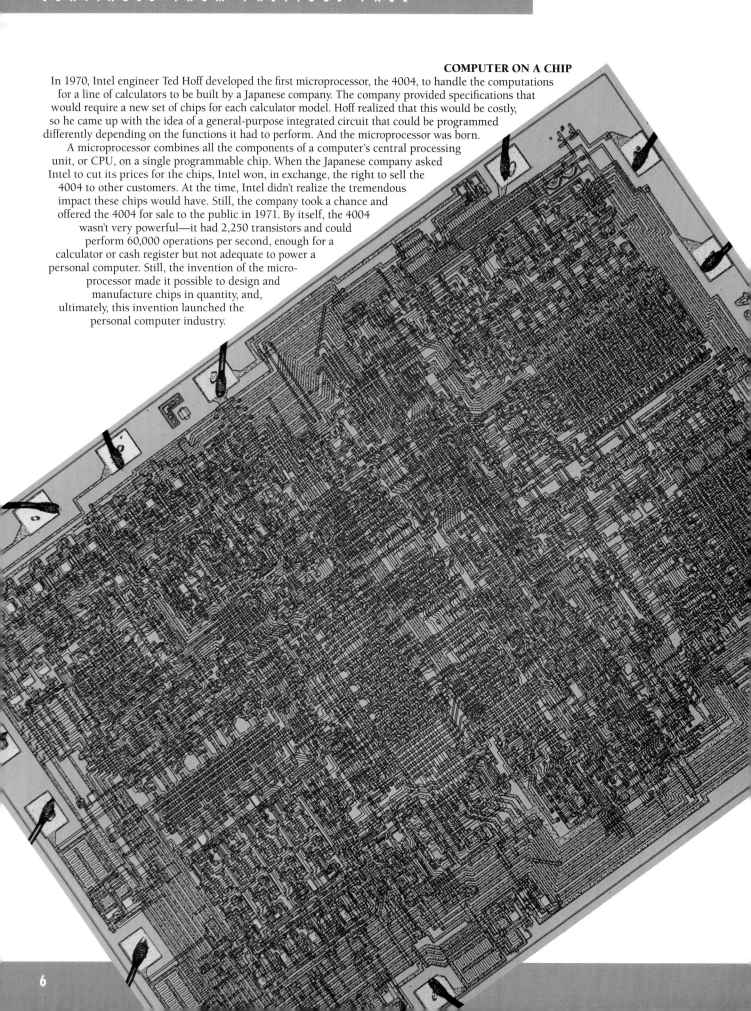

## ELECTRON TUBES AND TRANSISTORS

All operations in a computer rely on the transmission of electronic pulses. But special material is needed to control the computer's electrical charges as they travel through the machine. The equipment required to do this has changed dramatically since the first computers. Early computers such as ENIAC (lower right) used thousands of electron tubes like the one shown at left. Unfortunately, the tubes were fragile, tended to overheat, and were liable to burn out like ordinary light bulbs. In 1947, three scientists at Bell Telephone Company's laboratories developed the transistor (at right), which accomplished the same thing as an electron tube but lasted longer and was less expensive to make. Early transistors were composed of a sandwich of *silicon*, a semiconducting material made from sand. Semiconducting material neither lets electricity flow through it easily (as a conductor does) nor completely prevents electricity flow (as an insulator does). When specially treated layers of silicon are laid on top of each other in a transistor, the electrical current going through them can be controlled. Transistorized computers were smaller, faster, and more powerful than their tube-filled predecessors.

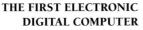

## INTEGRATED CIRCUITS

The development of the integrated circuit in the 1950s brought computer miniaturization to a new level. On a single piece of silicon, called a *chip*, the integrated circuit contained electrical components—transistors, resistors, capacitors—to form a complete electrical circuit. Wires were no longer needed to string the different components together. The circuit shown here, developed by Fairchild Instrument & Camera Company in 1961, is a logic circuit with two on-and-off switches. The blue or green arrow-shaped pieces in the center are transistors; the light lines are aluminum connectors. The device is about 1/16 of an inch in diameter.

## THE FIRST ELECTRONIC DIGITAL COMPUTER

This room-sized computer was developed in the 1940s to compute firing tables for U.S. Army artillery during World War II. Called ENIAC (for Electronic Numerical Integrator and Calculator), the machine could not store programs or remember more than 20 ten-digit numbers. Nevertheless, its speed was impressive. Performing 5,000 additions per second, ENIAC could calculate a weapon's trajectory, or angle, in 20 seconds. One of the "human computers" the Army had hired to do the calculations by hand took three days to accomplish the same task. ENIAC weighed 30 tons and used more than 18,000 vacuum tubes to transmit electrical signals.

# The Rise of the Personal Computer

With big, old computers, everyone had to share. The computer was too powerful and too expensive for any one person to own. If you wanted to use the computer, you had to make an appointment. You handed your computer program to one of the big computer's operators to run. If your program had problems, you couldn't fix them then; you had to make another appointment.

So, it's not surprising that people who needed computers in their work used to dream about being able to have a computer of their own. When the microprocessor made it possible to build smaller, cheaper computers, a dream was fulfilled. Although only as old as a high school student, the personal computer has already become one of the most important inventions in human history.

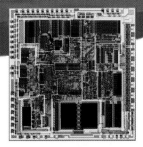

**80386**
**Introduced: 1985**
**Number of transistors: 275,000**

**80486**
**Introduced: 1989**
**Number of transistors: 1,200,000**

**80286**
**Introduced: 1982**
**Number of transistors: 130,000**

## THE EVOLUTION OF PERSONAL COMPUTING

Personal computers have come a long way in a short time. Computers easy and inexpensive enough for individuals to buy were first developed in the mid-1970s. Since then, they have become smaller, faster, and more powerful.

### 1975
**THE ALTAIR**
*Popular Electronics* magazine showcases the first so-called personal computer, the Altair 8800. Built from a kit, it's programmed via switches on the front panel.

### 1976
**THE APPLE I**
Apple Computer founders Steve Wozniak and Steve Jobs develop the Apple I, a pre-assembled computer circuit board. It has no keyboard, case, sound, or graphics.

### 1978
**THE FLOPPY DISK**
The floppy disk, a thin, round sheet of magnetic material in a flexible plastic case, replaces the cassette tape as the storage medium of choice.

### 1980
**THE HARD DISK**
Seagate Technology introduces the hard disk, a storage device that holds 5 megabytes of programs and data—30 times as much as the floppy disk. It fits in the same space as a floppy-disk drive.

### 1981
**MS-DOS**
Microsoft founder Bill Gates introduces MS-DOS (Microsoft Disk Operating System) as the operating system for the soon-to-be released IBM PC.

**Pentium**
**Introduced: 1993**
**Number of transistors:**
**3,100,000**

**8088**
**Introduced: 1979**
**Number of transistors:**
**29,000**

## THE EVOLUTION OF PC MICROPROCESSORS

It is impossible to talk about the evolution of the personal computer without discussing the evolution of PC microprocessors. These Intel chips show how far microprocessors have come in 15 years.

## PERSONAL COMPUTERS TODAY

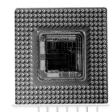

Your family may have bought a computer in a department store, at a flea market, or through the mail. Today's PCs are cheaper and easier to use than ever before. There are more programs to run on them, too, from simple games to CD encyclopedias with full-motion video and sound.

### 1981

#### THE IBM PC
IBM rolls out the IBM PC. With its policy of *open architecture*, IBM makes the hardware design available to anyone who wants to write software or build accessories for it, thereby adding lots of fuel to the PC business.

### 1983

#### THE COMPAQ PORTABLE COMPUTER
Compaq introduces its 28-pound portable computer, which has a hardware setup virtually identical to that of the IBM PC. In the years that follow, hundreds of other so-called compatibles or clones will be developed.

### 1984

#### THE APPLE MACINTOSH
Apple Computer launches the Macintosh. Hailed as the first popular graphical computer, the new machine has easy-to-use pull-down menus and a mouse-driven interface.

### 1990

#### WINDOWS 3.0
Microsoft introduces Windows 3.0, a mouse-driven environment that shields users from DOS's unfriendly command system. Within months, software developers debut hundreds of Windows programs. A subindustry is born.

### 1993

#### THE PENTIUM CHIP
Microprocessor giant Intel releases the Pentium chip, which contains a whopping 3.1 million transistors and operates more than twice as fast as its predecessor, the 80486.

# You Be the Microprocessor

The microprocessor made it possible to design computers that could do a variety of tasks depending on the software they were running. In this activity, you'll be the microprocessor. Using the listed hardware, run the software programs shown below. What are the results? (For the answers, see the key at the back of this book.)

Here's the basic hardware you'll need (only some of the hardware is required for each program):

| | |
|---|---|
| Eggs | Mixer |
| Flour | Baking sheet |
| Butter | Loaf pan |
| Sugar | Measuring spoons |
| Vanilla extract | Knife |
| Salt | Wooden spoon |
| Measuring cup | Skillet |
| Bowl | Oven/stove |

### Software Program 1
Preheat the oven to 375° F. Put ½ pound butter and 1 teaspoon vanilla in a bowl. Use a mixer to cream them together. Slowly add ⅔ cup sugar and 2 eggs and mix well. Mix 1½ cups flour and ½ teaspoon salt together and add them to the bowl, mixing thoroughly. Scoop out one teaspoonful at a time onto a baking sheet, leaving 2 inches between each one. Place in the middle rack of the oven for 8 minutes. Remove and cool.

### Software Program 2
Melt 1 tablespoon of butter in a skillet over medium heat. Crack two eggs into a bowl, add a pinch of salt, and beat slightly. When the butter stops bubbling, pour the contents of the bowl into the skillet. Stir with a wooden spoon for 2 to 3 minutes. Turn out onto a plate and garnish with parsley.

### Software Program 3
Preheat the oven to 325° F. Butter and flour a loaf pan. Cream ½ pound butter and 1⅔ cups sugar together until fluffy. Add 5 eggs, one at a time, blending well after each one. Stir in 2 cups flour, ½ teaspoon salt, and 1 teaspoon vanilla, and mix well. Spoon the mixture into the loaf pan and bake for 1¼ to 1½ hours. Remove from the oven, wait 5 minutes, and turn out onto a rack. Slice and serve.

# Make a Pebble Computer

The abacus was created as a way to calculate and store decimal numbers. A pebble computer, too, can be used in this way. A pebble computer consists of a series of concentric circles, one for each decimal place. The circles are similar to the rods on an abacus. Each circle can hold a pebble representing the number that belongs in that place.

It's easy to make your own pebble computer that can represent numbers into the thousands. All you need is a piece of chalk and four pebbles. (If you're stuck inside the house, you can use a pencil and paper instead.) First draw four concentric circles, and then draw nine dividing lines, as in the examples below. The innermost circle represents the 1s. If you put a pebble at the intersection of the innermost circle and the line that goes from the middle to the top of the computer, the amount is 1. As you move clockwise around the inner circle, you continue to count by 1, until you reach 9. After 9, you move the pebble out to the next circle, right above the 1. That represents the number 10. To make 11, you'd place one pebble in the 10 position and another in the 1 position. In the second circle, the next position to the right of the 10 is the 20, then the 30, and so on.

Here are some examples:

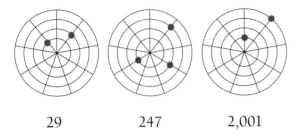

29          247          2,001

Now you can complete the following projects yourself. (For the answers, see the key at the back of this book.)

1. Draw in the following numbers in these blank pebble computers:

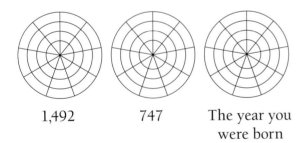

1,492          747          The year you were born

2. Make the following calculations with these blank pebble computers:

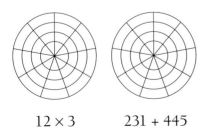

12 × 3          231 + 445

# Spell in Code

A computer uses electronic pulses to encode all kinds of information—numbers, letters, music, and pictures. It can't understand letters and music any better than you can understand electronic pulses. Yet a computer's dazzling speed allows it to instantly translate the information you send it into terms it understands and then send it back again.

Here's a scheme for encoding letters of the alphabet. A push-button telephone has numbers and letters arranged as shown to the right.

| 1 | 2 ABC | 3 DEF |
|---|-------|-------|
| 4 GHI | 5 JKL | 6 MNO |
| 7 PRS | 8 TUV | 9 WXY |
| * | 0 OPER | # |

The code is simple: The letter you want to use is represented by the number of the phone key it's on, followed by the number—1, 2, or 3—which describes the position of the letter in the series. So 52 represents the letter *K* and 41 represents the letter *G*. You can use the code to spell anything that doesn't have the letters *Q* or *Z*.

1. What do the following phrases say? (For the answers, see the key at the back of this book.)

   23-63-61-71-82-81-32-72-73  21-72-32 23-63-63-53

   62-63-91 43  52-62-63-91  61-93 21-22-23-73

2. Write your name in the code.

# How Computers Solve Problems

Computers and people are very different from one another, but they solve problems in similar ways. This is not surprising since, after all, computers must follow the rules people give them. When you solve a problem, you need information—that's the meat of the problem. You need a method—that's the way you solve the problem. You produce a result—that's the output of your work. Thus, at the most basic level, when you solve a problem—say, multiplying 6 × 8— you're acting like a computer. Here's how the computer's processing of information compares with your "processing" of a simple math problem.

**INPUT**
Before it can process anything, the computer needs to get its marching orders. This is accomplished via *input*, the data that goes into the computer. The most common input devices are the keyboard and the mouse. Likewise, you use your senses—sight, hearing, taste, smell, and touch—to gather information from the world around you.

**CLOCK**
A computer's clock beats at thousands of pulses per second to make sure that all its components are acting at the same speed. Likewise, your heart beats constantly to keep your vital organs supplied with blood.

**POWER SUPPLY**
Without electricity or some other source of power— such as a battery—the computer can't generate the electronic pulses that it needs to process data. In th same way, you need energy—which your body gets from food—to solve a problem or do any other task

## MEMORY

Without memory, the computer wouldn't know how to act on the information it receives or be able to remember what the result is. Personal computer memory comes in two forms: *internal memory*, which contains data and instructions that the computer has instantly at its disposal, and *external memory*, which acts as permanent storage for information that the computer needs only occasionally. A computer's internal memory is like the memory you use to solve easy problems or answer easy questions. The computer's external memory is more like a library that you can refer to when you need to look up information that you don't know by heart.

## OUTPUT

Once the computer has accepted the instructions and processed the information, it uses output as a way to communicate the result back to the user. The most common output devices are the screen and printer. Your output might take the form of speech or writing.

## PROCESSOR

The microprocessor is the control center of the computer. It collects the input, sends it to the correct location for processing, calculates the result and stores it in memory, and sends the result to be output. Your brain gathers information from the outside world, processes it, and remembers it in a similar fashion.

# Inside a Computer Box

The personal computer is a marvel of miniaturization and efficiency. The computing power now packed into the personal computer's inch-square microprocessor required a gymnasium full of equipment just 40 years ago. The memory squeezed onto fingernail-tiny chips used to overflow row upon row of refrigerator-sized storage units. Today, not only is the personal computer small, it is inexpensive. Two decades ago, all computers cost millions of dollars each. Today, a personal computer powerful enough to do the work of any of those old machines costs less than a thousand dollars. Never in human history has an invention improved in price and performance so quickly. To get a sense of the change, compare PCs to cars: Twenty years ago, a top-of-the-line car cost $10,000, got 20 miles per gallon of gas, weighed a couple of tons, and could reach speeds up to 100 miles per hour. If that car had improved as fast as a PC, today it would cost $100, get 2,000 miles per gallon, weigh 100 pounds, and achieve speeds of 10,000 miles per hour.

### INSIDE AN IBM-COMPATIBLE PC

Today's ordinary PC packs hundreds of times the problem-solving power of old room-sized computers into a box the size of a briefcase. You can see here some of the parts common to every computer: the power supply, for giving the PC the energy it needs; the microprocessor, also known as the CPU (central processing unit), which coordinates all the activities that go on inside the machine; the memory chips, which store information while the PC is working on it; the hard disk, where information can be stored permanently; and the cards, which are plug-in components that give the computer extra functions, such as the ability to send faxes or to make a variety of sounds.

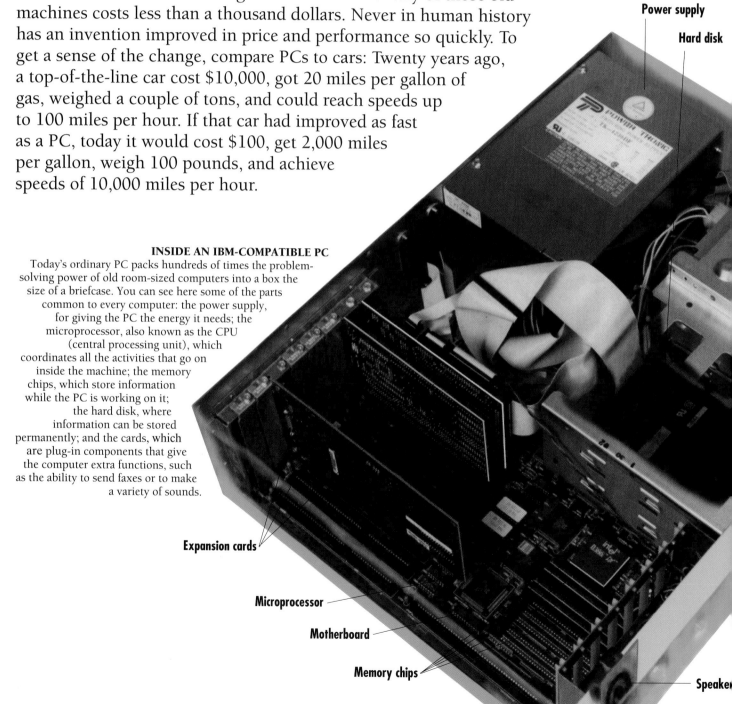

Power supply

Hard disk

Expansion cards

Microprocessor

Motherboard

Memory chips

Speaker

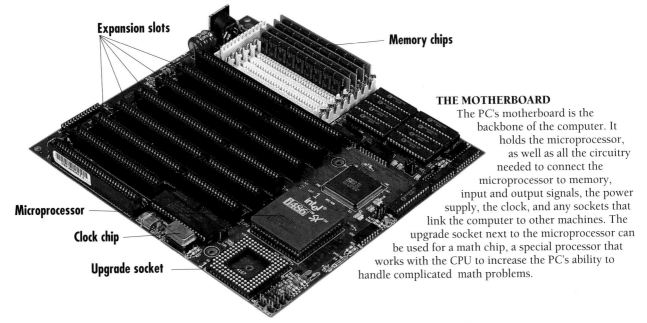

**Expansion slots**

**Memory chips**

**Microprocessor**

**Clock chip**

**Upgrade socket**

### THE MOTHERBOARD

The PC's motherboard is the backbone of the computer. It holds the microprocessor, as well as all the circuitry needed to connect the microprocessor to memory, input and output signals, the power supply, the clock, and any sockets that link the computer to other machines. The upgrade socket next to the microprocessor can be used for a math chip, a special processor that works with the CPU to increase the PC's ability to handle complicated math problems.

### THE POWER SUPPLY

Ever wonder what makes that whirring noise when your computer is turned on? It's the power supply—or, more specifically, the fan inside the power supply that keeps the PC's "engine" from overheating.

### THE WELL-CONNECTED COMPUTER

The sockets on the back of a PC are its connection to the outside world. These connectors, or ports, channel input and output between the PC and the keyboard, monitor, printer, modem, and other devices. Not all ports operate in the same way. A serial port works like a telegraph key, either sending or receiving one bit of data at a time. Most commonly it is used to connect the PC to a mouse or modem. If a serial port is like a one-lane road, a parallel port is like a highway. It handles data side by side, 8 bits at a time. This means a parallel port can send more information than a serial port can in the same amount of time, and it can receive and send information at the same time. Parallel ports are used most often to connect the PC to a printer. That's because printing requires a lot of data to be sent from the PC to the printer at the same time that the printer is sending information (such as "I'm out of paper") to the PC.

**Fan**

**Serial ports**

**Video port**

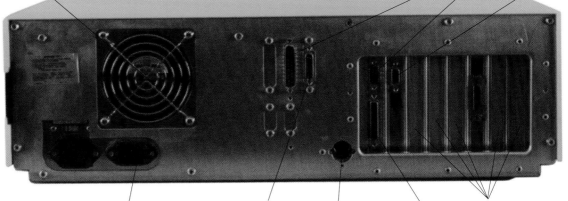

**Power-supply connector**     **Game port**     **Keyboard port**     **Parallel port**     **Unused expansion slots**

# Memory and Storage

Imagine how frustrating computers would be if they couldn't remember anything: To add 2 and 2, you would have to type in the first number, all the rules for adding, and the second number as fast as the computer could process them—an impossible task. Finding a way for the computer to hold onto the information it needs to solve problems has been a central issue in computing. Many different methods have been tried, using everything from numbered gears to vacuum tubes to today's high-speed memory chips.

But what if you want the computer to repeat the same process many times with different information? Or make a permanent record of an answer to a question? This requires a longer-lasting method of retaining information—it requires some kind of physical storage. Memory is essential for computers, but storage, though enormously important, is an option. In fact, early modern computers had no storage: You typed in your problem, the computer gave you an answer, and you wrote it down and left. Since then, computers have used many kinds of storage, including paper cards with punched holes and big spools of magnetic recording tape. Today, computers can store on a palm-sized circle of plastic as much information as once filled roomfuls of storage cabinets.

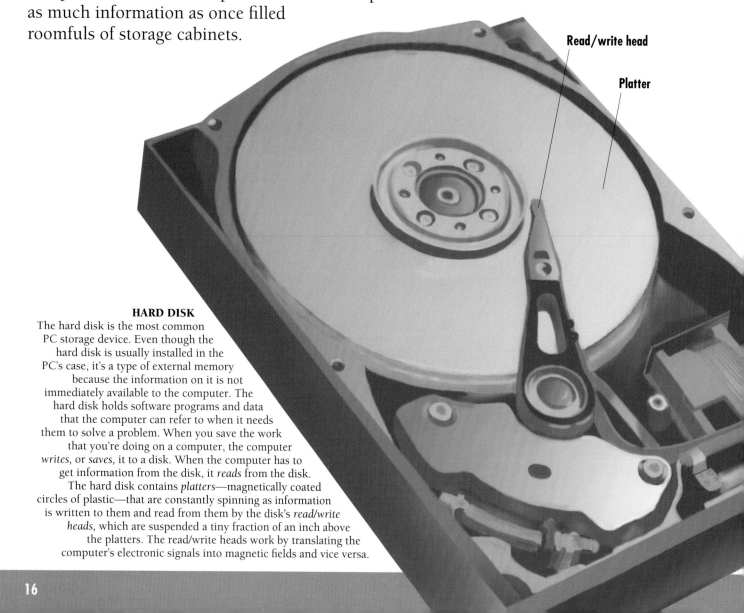

**Read/write head**

**Platter**

### HARD DISK

The hard disk is the most common PC storage device. Even though the hard disk is usually installed in the PC's case, it's a type of external memory because the information on it is not immediately available to the computer. The hard disk holds software programs and data that the computer can refer to when it needs them to solve a problem. When you save the work that you're doing on a computer, the computer *writes*, or *saves*, it to a disk. When the computer has to get information from the disk, it *reads* from the disk. The hard disk contains *platters*—magnetically coated circles of plastic—that are constantly spinning as information is written to them and read from them by the disk's *read/write heads*, which are suspended a tiny fraction of an inch above the platters. The read/write heads work by translating the computer's electronic signals into magnetic fields and vice versa.

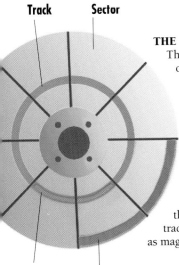

Track    Sector

Cluster    FAT

## THE PC'S LIBRARY

The computer organizes information on a hard disk and on a floppy disk in similar ways. Can you imagine trying to look up something in the library without using a card catalog or database? With the vast amount of information that can be stored on a disk, the computer needs a catalog, too. Every disk contains a *file allocation table,* or FAT, which is a magnetically encoded directory of the information on the disk. The FAT tells the computer where it can find a file in terms of tracks and sectors. *Sectors* are pie-slice sections of the disk or platter, and *tracks* are circular subsections of the disk. Two or more sector slices on the same track make up a *cluster.* You can't see the FAT, tracks, sectors, or clusters on a real disk. They exist only as magnetic fields that the drive's read/write heads can read.

## MEMORY CHIPS

A PC's internal memory comes in two forms: *random-access memory,* or RAM, and *read-only memory,* or ROM. Both types of memory are stored on chips. A ROM chip holds basic information and programs that the computer always needs at its disposal. ROM is

**ROM chip**

permanent memory that can't be changed. One of the most important programs stored in a PC's ROM is the *basic input/output system,* or BIOS. The BIOS tells the computer what to do when it's turned on and contains basic functions for routing input and output signals, such as taking keystrokes (input) and translating them into characters on the screen (output). RAM chips, on the other hand, are the computer's temporary memory: From the moment you turn on your

## FLOPPY DISKS

A floppy disk, or floppy, stores information in the same way as a hard disk. But a floppy disk contains only one circle of magnetically coated plastic, encased in a protective plastic sleeve. And you need a separate drive, with its own read/write head, to read or write information on a floppy disk. PC floppies come in two sizes: 5¼ inches and 3½ inches. They can't hold as much data as a hard disk can, but they're convenient because they're so portable; you can pop a floppy into any compatible computer drive and get access to the information on it.

**RAM chips**

computer, everything it does is based on information stored in and drawn from RAM. Both you and the computer can change what's in RAM. The computer changes the contents of RAM with every step of a problem it solves. You change the contents of RAM every time you enter information into the computer. RAM chips can accept and offer information very fast, but they can hold information only while the PC is turned on because they require an electrical charge to work. As soon as you turn off the machine, whatever was in RAM disappears. That's why it's important to save your work if you want to refer back to it later.

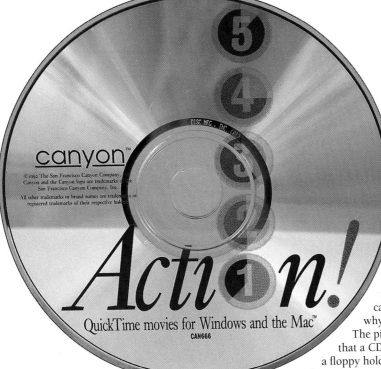

## CD-ROM STORAGE

Compact disc read-only memory (CD-ROM) is another kind of external PC memory. Like a hard or floppy disk, a CD-ROM disc can hold information that the computer can refer to whenever it needs it. Whereas a hard disk uses a read/write head to translate magnetic fields into electronic pulses, the CD-ROM drive uses a laser beam to read and translate microscopic pits on the surface of the disc. You can't change the data on a CD-ROM disc (that's why it's called *CD-ROM,* for read-only memory). The pits are so tiny, and the laser beam is so precise, that a CD-ROM can hold more than 600 times what a floppy holds. That's why you'll find encyclopedias and other reference materials on CD-ROM discs.

# Input and Output

EOWW!

To use a computer, we must have a method for getting information and instructions into the machine. We also need some way of receiving the computer's answer. Looking at your PC, you might think that computers have always used mice, keyboards, and video screens. They seem like such natural ways to enter information, which is known as *input,* and to get information from the computer, known as *output.* The first modern computers actually required wires to be plugged into circuit boards for input. To get the computer to create the letter *A,* for example, you couldn't type the letter on the keyboard—you had to actually wire that circuit. As for output, there weren't any attractive graphics screens then, either. Answers were represented in rows of lights (you've probably seen them in old sci-fi movies). Today's input methods are much more natural, which is why so many more people can use computers comfortably.

And when it comes to output, we have video screens and printers that can present us with vast amounts of information and great-looking pictures, too.

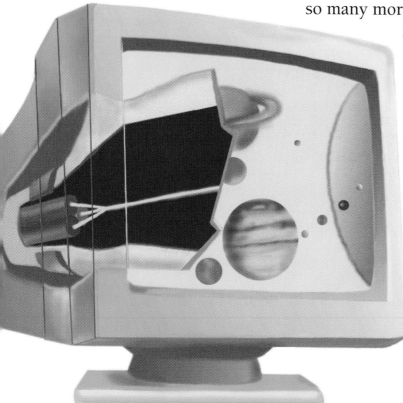

### MONITOR

A PC's monitor is its most important output device. It gives you immediate feedback about what's going on inside the computer, whether it's receiving letters you type in at the keyboard, controlling another piece of equipment such as a printer or modem, or simply waiting for further instructions. Information that needs to be displayed visually is sent to the monitor through a video adapter. A video adapter converts electrical signals from the CPU into tiny points of color, called *pixels,* that together form an image on the screen. The monitor can generate only three colors—red, green, and blue—but by mixing them in different amounts, it allows the screen to display millions of colors for you to see.

### ESCAPE KEY

The *Escape key* often causes a program to go back to where it was before you made the previous selection or gave the previous command.

### KEYBOARD

The keyboard is the most common computer input device. It's usually the first stop for the commands you use to tell the computer to start a game, show letters and numbers on the screen, save your work, print a page, and so on. In addition to letters, numbers, and punctuation marks, a computer keyboard has special keys to help you control it. Not all keyboards have the same keys in the same positions, but this is the layout of a typical QWERTY keyboard (named for the first five letter keys in the upper left-hand corner).

### CTRL AND ALT KEYS

By using the *Ctrl* and *Alt* keys in combination with other keys, you're able to send a greater variety of commands to the computer. For example, pressing the Alt key and the H key at the same time often summons instructions for the program you're using.

## MOUSE

The most popular alternative to the keyboard for input is the mouse, a hand-held plastic device with two or three buttons at your fingertips and a ball underneath that rolls to control the movement of the PC's on-screen cursor. When you move the mouse to the right, the cursor moves to the right, too. If you press, or click, on the left button once you've positioned the cursor over a command on the screen, the mouse acts like the keyboard's Enter key, carrying out whatever instruction you clicked on. Many programs, including drawing and desktop publishing programs, can be controlled much more easily with a mouse than with a keyboard.

## PRINTER

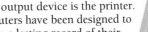

Next to a monitor, the most popular output device is the printer. Computers have been designed to make a lasting record of their results since the Analytical Engine (see the chapter, "Where Did Computers Come From?"). Printers can record data with tiny bubbles of ink, with an inked ribbon, with crayonlike blocks of wax, or with black powder that's fused to paper with heat. For more on printing, see the next chapter.

## BAR-CODE READER

You've seen bar codes on all sorts of products, from toys to food to magazines. A bar-code reader is another kind of computer input device. The bar-code reader uses a laser beam to scan the lines and spaces in the code and then translate them into a series of numbers. The most common bar code is the Universal Product Code (UPC), in which certain combinations of lines and spaces always represent certain digits. Once the bar-code reader's digitizer sends the number to the computer, the software matches the number to a record with the product's name, price, and other information.

## FUNCTION KEYS

The *function keys* give you shortcuts for telling the PC to do certain things, depending on the software it's running. For example, pressing the F1 function key often tells the computer to show you a screen with instructions on how to use the program you're using.

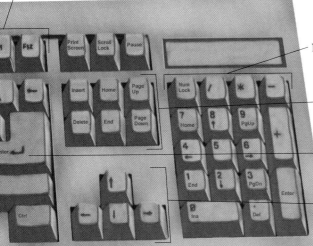

## NUMERIC KEYPAD

The *numeric keypad* is a block of keys that makes it easy to do calculations— to a computer, the / stands for division and the * stands for multiplication.

## TEXT-EDITING KEYS

The block of keys for text editing makes it easy to move around in and edit documents.

## ENTER KEY

The *Enter key* is the most important of the PC's special keys: You often use it to tell the computer to carry out an instruction you've typed.

## CURSOR KEYS

The cursor keys help you move the cursor on the screen. The *cursor* is a little block or bar on the monitor that indicates where you are in a program.

# Printers

If computers couldn't transfer their information onto paper and make it portable, permanent, and in a form that's common around the world, they wouldn't be very useful. Getting a mighty machine like a computer to print letters and draw lines may seem simple, but, in fact, printing is one of the hardest tasks a computer must do. That's because a computer is *electronic*—that is, it works by moving tiny electrical pulses at nearly the speed of light—but a printer is *mechanical,* operating by force being applied to physical machinery. Computers are good at moving little bits of an electrical charge around at incredible speeds, but printing demands the physical placement of ink on paper, and the computer has to be trained, by software, in every aspect of that mechanical process. What's more, the mechanical work of the printer is so slow, compared to the computer's lightning speed, that clever ways must be found to keep the computer and printer in sync. From the moment you tell the printer to print until the paper rolls into your hand, a lot has to happen.

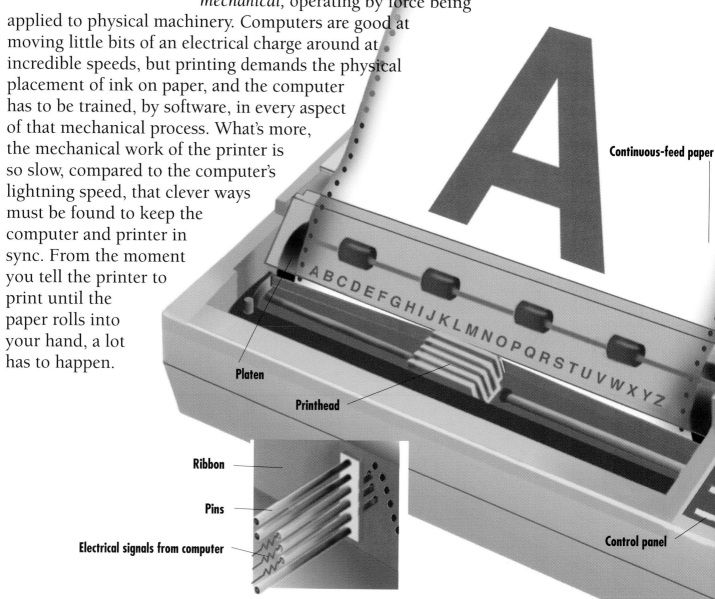

Continuous-feed paper

Platen

Printhead

Ribbon

Pins

Electrical signals from computer

Control panel

## GETTING IT ON PAPER

There are many methods for getting information from inside a computer onto a printed page, but the most popular way is with a dot-matrix printer. A dot-matrix printer contains a printhead with a vertical column of tiny pins. The computer sends signals to the individual pins as the printhead moves across the page, causing the pins to press against an inked ribbon and make dots on the paper. Together, the dots form the letters and pictures that end up on the printed page. Like most printers, a dot-matrix printer is actually a special-purpose computer dedicated to the task of printing on paper: It accepts input (signals from the computer), keeps data in memory (to hold information about the characters to be printed), processes the data (by determining which pins to press), and generates output (the printed page).

 **cyan** **magenta**
**yellow**
 **black**

## COLOR PRINTING

Believe it or not, color printers can actually print only four colors. By overlapping dots of different intensities and colors, a color printer, like a professional printing press, can create thousands of colors from just cyan, magenta, yellow, and black. Color printers translate images from the computer onto paper through colored ribbons, colored ink, or crayonlike blocks of wax that are melted onto the page.

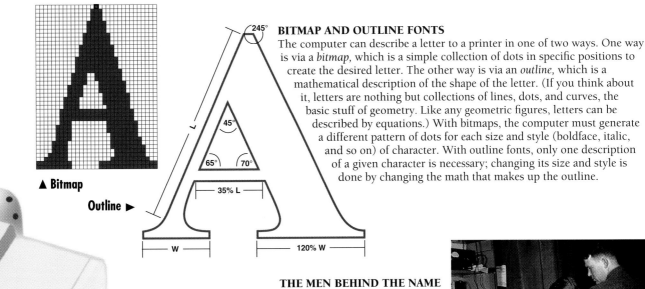

▲ **Bitmap**

**Outline** ▶

## BITMAP AND OUTLINE FONTS

The computer can describe a letter to a printer in one of two ways. One way is via a *bitmap,* which is a simple collection of dots in specific positions to create the desired letter. The other way is via an *outline,* which is a mathematical description of the shape of the letter. (If you think about it, letters are nothing but collections of lines, dots, and curves, the basic stuff of geometry. Like any geometric figures, letters can be described by equations.) With bitmaps, the computer must generate a different pattern of dots for each size and style (boldface, italic, and so on) of character. With outline fonts, only one description of a given character is necessary; changing its size and style is done by changing the math that makes up the outline.

## THE MEN BEHIND THE NAME

One of the world's biggest printer companies is the Hewlett-Packard Company. In 1938, William Hewlett (standing) and David Packard—two electrical engineers from Stanford University—started the company out of their garage in Palo Alto, California, with $538. Hewlett-Packard was founded to develop and sell electronic testing and measuring equipment. As the years went by, the company kept up with the times and helped pioneer the personal computing industry. Today Hewlett-Packard is the world's dominant laser printer manufacturer.

## FASTER AND QUIETER

Next to dot-matrix printers, laser printers are the most popular choice for printed output. And it's no wonder—they're fast, quiet, and create great-looking pages. In a laser printer, computer signals are translated into pulses in a small laser light. Turning on and off millions of times each second, the laser light bounces off a mirror, which reflects the light onto a cylindrical drum. Where ink should appear, the laser focuses on pinpoint spots across the drum's surface, magnetizing them. As the drum turns, a fine black powder, called toner, sticks to the magnetized areas of the drum. Then a sheet of paper with a small magnetic charge passes under the drum and attracts the toner. Finally, the printed image is fused to the paper as it passes through a set of heated rollers.

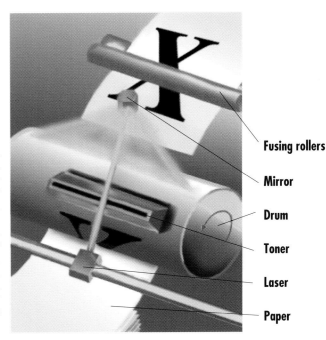

**Fusing rollers**

**Mirror**

**Drum**

**Toner**

**Laser**

**Paper**

## How RAM Works

A computer's software keeps track of what's stored in random-access memory, or RAM, through a system of addresses that contain signals that the computer can understand. Each memory address contains what's known as a *word*, which in modern PCs can consist of 8 bits, 16 bits, or 32 bits. When the CPU needs a certain piece of information, the computer's software looks it up by its address and delivers it.

In this project, you are the software in control of fetching the data and giving it to the microprocessor. The words are English words instead of binary codes. The addresses are expressed with letters and numbers. And the "processing" that's being done is you simply connecting the words into a phrase. You can make up your own phrases using the address table below, too.

|   | A | B | C | D |
|---|---|---|---|---|
| 1 | EARNED | PENNY | IS | FOOL |
| 2 | AND | HIS | ARE | PARTED |
| 3 | RACE | A | WITH | SAVED |
| 4 | SLOW | THE | WINS | FOREVER |
| 5 | MAN'S | ANOTHER | WHOEVER | DIES |
| 6 | SOON | MOST | CEILING | THING |
| 7 | OF | ONE | MONEY | JOY |
| 8 | TOYS | FLOOR | BEAUTY | STEADY |

Here are the addresses of the words that the CPU is asking you to fetch:

B3 D1 A2 B2 C7 C2 A6 D2.

B3 B1 D3 C1 B3 B1 A1.

A4 A2 D8 C4 B4 A3.

C5 D5 C3 B4 B6 A8 C4.

B7 A5 C6 C1 B5 A5 B8.

B3 D6 A7 C8 C1 B3 D7 D4.

(For the answers, see the key at the back of this book.)

## You Be the Printer

As you saw in the "Printers" chapter, dot-matrix printers can create an endless variety of letters and graphics by putting different arrangements of dots on the page. In this project, you'll create an image on paper by following the instructions below (which are similar to the instructions the computer sends to the printer).

On a sheet of graph paper, outline a box that's 20 squares high by 35 squares wide. Label the squares along the side with the letters of the alphabet, A through T. Label the squares along the top with the numbers 1 through 35.

Now follow these instructions for filling in the squares, working from left to right in each letter row. (For the answer, see the key at the back of this book.)

A —
B 10, 16, 18, 31
C 5, 10, 16, 18, 28, 31
D 4–6, 11, 15, 18, 20, 24, 25, 28, 29, 33–35
E 3–7, 11, 13, 15, 18, 19, 21, 26, 28, 32
F 2–8, 11, 13, 15, 18, 21, 24–26, 28, 33, 34
G 5, 12, 14, 18, 21, 23, 26, 28, 35
H 5, 12, 14, 18, 21, 24–26, 29, 32–34
I 5
J 5, 29, 30
K 5, 7–15, 28, 31
L 5, 7, 15, 18, 21, 23–25, 31
M 5, 7, 9–13, 15, 18, 21, 23, 26, 30
N 5, 7, 9, 13, 15, 18, 21, 23, 26, 29
O 5, 7, 9, 11, 13, 15, 18, 21, 23, 26
P 5, 7, 9–11, 13, 15, 19–21, 23–25, 29
Q 5, 7, 13, 15, 23
R 5, 7–13, 15, 23
S 5, 15
T 5–15

# Make a Fortune-Telling Computer

With a piece of paper, some colored pencils or highlighters, and a pen, you can make a fortune-telling computer that demonstrates the principles of input, memory, processing, and output.

1. Start with a square piece of paper, about 8 inches by 8 inches. Fold and unfold the paper in half from top to bottom and from side to side. Use colored pencils to lightly fill in the four smaller squares made by the fold marks.

2. Turn over the paper (so the colored part is facing down) and fold each corner into the center. You now have a smaller square, with four colored triangles facing you.

3. Turn over the paper again, so the folded corners are facing down. Now fold each corner of the smaller square into the center to make an even smaller square.

4. Bring all four new corners up to meet each other and push out the loose corners to make flaps, like this:

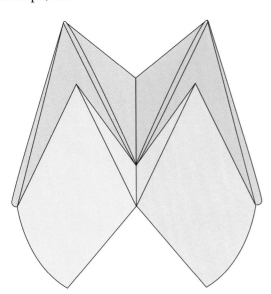

5. Now you're ready to load up your computer's *"memory."* You have room for eight fortunes. Write them in, two under each inner triangular flap. The fortunes should answer a yes or no question, for example:

> Absolutely.
> Forget it.
> Maybe.
> Try again with another color.
> Yes, but only if you…

6. Fold the fortune-teller back up with the points facing up. Put your thumbs and index fingers into the four pockets created by the flaps. Now you can move your fingers so the points separate from side to side or from top to bottom, each time exposing four colored triangles inside.

7. Now you have it, a fortune-telling computer! Have a friend ask you a question that can be answered by yes or no. This is the *input*.

8. Spell out your friend's name. With each letter, open the fortune teller from side to side or top to bottom. This is the *processing* and you are the power supply.

9. When you get to the last letter of the name, ask your friend to choose a color. Then lift the flap of that color and read the fortune beneath. This is the *output*.

# Binary Basics

Computers are collections of tiny switches called transistors. As electronic pulses travel through a computer, these transistors, like all switches, are either on or off. The computer stores information by setting transistors into specific on-off patterns. Because today's computers have millions of transistors, they can hold extremely complex patterns of on-off switches, transforming these two simple signals into information of all kinds—not only letters and numbers, but also animated pictures or stereo sounds. By changing the pattern of switches at blazing speed, a modern computer can handle difficult chores—anything from finding the average score of everyone who took this year's SAT test to recreating the Mona Lisa and then making her eyes blue. Whatever the task, though, all the computer actually does is turn switches on and off.

**A SIMPLE SYSTEM**
A computer's on-off switches are translated into a form people can understand through a binary number system. In a binary system, "on" is equivalent to 1 and "off" is equivalent to 0. Since its switches have only two options, a system for describing the pattern of a computer's transistors must use these two numbers exclusively. Just as in the decimal number system we use every day, each place in a binary number

| Decimal Number | Binary Numbers | What the Computer Does | Decimal Number | Binary Numbers | What the Computer Does |
|---|---|---|---|---|---|
| 1 | 0001 | | 5 | 0101 | |
| 2 | 0010 | | 6 | 0110 | |
| 3 | 0011 | | 7 | 0111 | |
| 4 | 0100 | | 8 | 1000 | |

represents a higher value. But instead of increasing by ten times as you move from right to left, binary numbers increase by only two times. Binary numbers get very long very quickly, but always with strings of 1s and 0s. These long numbers are easy for the computer to handle with its huge array of switches.

## MORSE CODE

One of the most widely used coding systems in the previous century, and a forerunner of ASCII, was the Morse code, developed by Samuel F. B. Morse. Morse created the code in 1838 as a way of transmitting messages over the telegraph. In Morse code, letters and numbers are represented by a series of audible short and long signals (dots and dashes). A telegraph operator would send the signals through a wire, causing an electromagnet to press down for either a very short period (a dot) or a somewhat longer period (a dash). The audible clicking of the magnet could be translated into the message by a telegraph operator on the other end. Perhaps the most familiar expression in Morse Code is the SOS distress signal, which translates into three dots (S), three dashes (O), and three dots (S).

## BITS AND BYTES

A *bit*—short for *binary digit*—is the smallest unit of information a computer can understand. A *byte* consists of 8 bits, and it is a common unit of measurement for a PC's memory and storage. The byte has been a useful unit of information since the development of micro-computers in the 1970s. Because early microcomputer memory chips could hold 8 bits at a given location in memory—known as the *memory address*—an international standard of 8-bit codes for representing letters, punctuation marks, and other input keys was developed—the ASCII code. The total amount of temporary memory and data storage that a PC has is usually measured in mega-bytes, which are units of a million bytes each. Many home computers today have 8 or more megabytes of RAM—that's more than one hundred times the memory of the computers that sent the first astronauts to the moon!

| | |
|---|---|
| A | 0 1 0 0 0 0 0 1 |
| B | 0 1 0 0 0 0 1 0 |
| C | 0 1 0 0 0 0 1 1 |
| D | 0 1 0 0 0 1 0 0 |
| E | 0 1 0 0 0 1 0 1 |
| F | 0 1 0 0 0 1 1 0 |
| G | 0 1 0 0 0 1 1 1 |
| H | 0 1 0 0 1 0 0 0 |
| I | 0 1 0 0 1 0 0 1 |
| J | 0 1 0 0 1 0 1 0 |
| K | 0 1 0 0 1 0 1 1 |
| L | 0 1 0 0 1 1 0 0 |
| M | 0 1 0 0 1 1 0 1 |
| N | 0 1 0 0 1 1 1 0 |
| O | 0 1 0 0 1 1 1 1 |
| P | 0 1 0 1 0 0 0 0 |
| Q | 0 1 0 1 0 0 0 1 |
| R | 0 1 0 1 0 0 1 0 |
| S | 0 1 0 1 0 0 1 1 |
| T | 0 1 0 1 0 1 0 0 |
| U | 0 1 0 1 0 1 0 1 |
| V | 0 1 0 1 0 1 1 0 |
| W | 0 1 0 1 0 1 1 1 |
| X | 0 1 0 1 1 0 0 0 |
| Y | 0 1 0 1 1 0 0 1 |
| Z | 0 1 0 1 1 0 1 0 |

## THE BINARY ALPHABET

The American Standard Code for Information Interchange, commonly known as ASCII, was developed in 1968 to present a universal way of encoding letters and numbers in binary form. Because it's an 8-bit system, ASCII can represent up to 256 charac-ters (binary 00000000 through 11111111—enough to hold the 26 letters of the alphabet, the digits 0 through 9, punctuation marks, graphics characters, and a variety of control keys such as you'll find on a typical computer keyboard.

## MUSIC TO THE EARS

Any information that can be *digitized*—that is, expressed as a collection of separate on-off signals—can be encoded in binary form. That includes music, as illustrated by this representation of the first four notes of Beethoven's Fifth Symphony. Music on a compact disc is digitized, as are the video images on a videotape. Any information that can be expressed in binary code can be processed and stored by a computer.

If programmers had to retrain the computer in every basic task every time they created software, programming would be incredibly hard, and using a computer would be very confusing. And, your computer would run completely differently with each program! To avoid this situation, special-purpose programs called operating systems have been created.

An *operating system* is a program that directs the basic housekeeping chores that a computer requires to run. It gets power to all the computer's hardware, moves data into and out of memory, sends computer signals to appropriate peripherals, and generally keeps track of what's going on inside the machine. The operating system provides these essential services in the same way to any program that runs on the computer. The operating system used on most of today's PCs is the Microsoft Disk Operating System, or DOS for short.

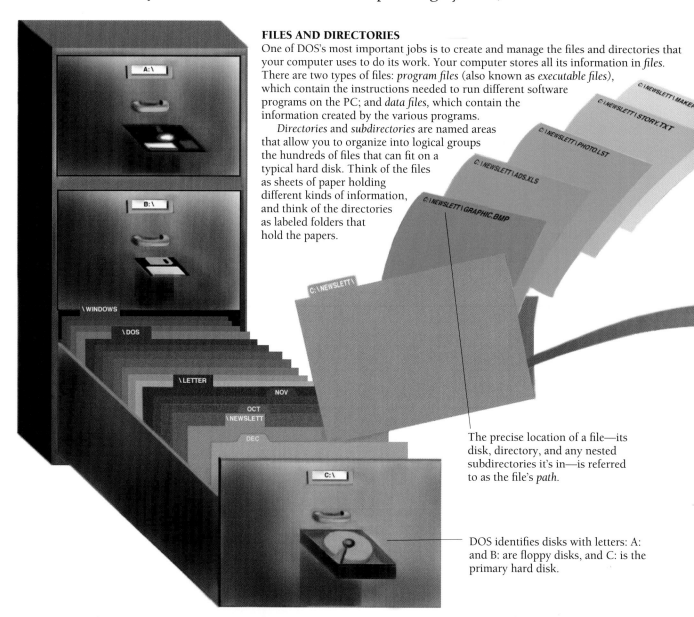

**FILES AND DIRECTORIES**

One of DOS's most important jobs is to create and manage the files and directories that your computer uses to do its work. Your computer stores all its information in *files*. There are two types of files: *program files* (also known as *executable files*), which contain the instructions needed to run different software programs on the PC; and *data files*, which contain the information created by the various programs.

*Directories* and *subdirectories* are named areas that allow you to organize into logical groups the hundreds of files that can fit on a typical hard disk. Think of the files as sheets of paper holding different kinds of information, and think of the directories as labeled folders that hold the papers.

The precise location of a file—its disk, directory, and any nested subdirectories it's in—is referred to as the file's *path*.

DOS identifies disks with letters: A: and B: are floppy disks, and C: is the primary hard disk.

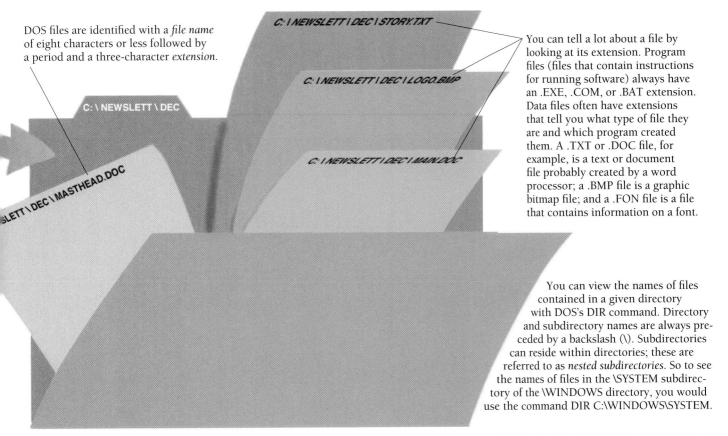

```
⌐±  Object    Edit    Link    View    Info    Tools    Quit           F1=Help
⌐Cluster 39, Sector 679
00000000:  E9 5D 14 00 78 14 00 00 - B7 0E 00 00 75 0D 00 00  θ]¶.x¶..┐.η...u♪..
00000010:  85 11 00 00 00 00 00 00 - 00 00 00 00 00 00 00 00  à◄..............
00000020:  00 00 00 00 00 00 00 00 - 00 00 00 00 00 00 00 00  ................
00000030:  00 00 00 00 00 FB E8 64 - 00 1E 0E 2E FF 2E 04 01  .....√Φd.▲...▌.☺
00000040:  FB E8 59 00 1E 0E 2E FF - 2E 08 01 FB E8 4E 00 1E  √ΦY.▲...▌.☺√ΦN.▲
00000050:  0E 2E FF 2E 0C 01 FB E8 - 43 00 1E 0E 2E FF 2E 10  .▲...▌.√ΦC.▲...►
00000060:  01 E8 39 00 1E 0E 2E FF - 2E 14 01 E8 2F 00 1E 0E  ☺Φ9.▲.....¶Φ/.▲.
00000070:  2E FF 2E 18 01 E8 25 00 - 1E 0E 2E FF 2E 1C 01 E8  .▌.↑ΦΘ%.▲....∟☺Φ
00000080:  1B 00 1E 0E 2E FF 2E 20 - 01 E8 11 00 1E 0E 2E FF  ←.▲... Θ◄.▲...▌
00000090:  2E 24 01 E8 07 00 1E 0E - 2E FF 2E 28 01 9C 2E 80  .$☺Φ•.▲...(ⁿ£.Ç
000000A0:  3E 34 01 00 74 08 E8 0C - 00 73 03 E8 1A 00 9D C3  >4☺.t◘Φ♀.s♥Φ→.¥├
000000B0:  EA 35 01 00 00 53 50 B4 - 07 2E FF 1E 30 01 0B C0  Ω5☺...SP┤•.▌.0☺♂└
000000C0:  58 5B 75 02 F9 C3 F8 C3 - 53 50 B4 05 2E FF 1E 30  X[u☻•▌°├SP┤♣.▌.0
000000D0:  01 0B C0 74 03 58 5B C3 - EB FE CD 21 FA 0E 17 BC  ☺♂└t♥X[├δ■.!.∙↨╝
000000E0:  3E 05 FB 0E 1F 9C 2E A0 - 40 05 A8 80 74 07 24 7F  >.√.▼£.áⁿ@.¿Çt•$⌂
000000F0:  2E FF 1E 2C 01 2E 80 26 - 40 05 7F 9D E9 62 FF 02  .▌.,☺.Ç&@.⌂ⁿΘbᵕ☻
00000100:  00 00 01 05 02 41 02 00 - 00 02 0C 02 00 00 00 00  ..☺♣☻A☻...☻♀☻....
00000110:  00 00 00 00 00 02 1E 02 - 03 2C 02 03 2A 02 00 00  .....☻▲☻♥,☻♥*☻..
00000120:  00 00 00 00 00 00 00 00 - 00 00 00 00 00 00 00 01  ...............☺
00000130:  05 02 02 00 00 01 38 02 - 20 02 69 04 00 00 00 00  ♣☻☻..☺8☻ ☻i♦....
└◆ File                                                         Cluster 39  ▲
   C:\\command.com                                          Offset 0, hex 0  ▼
Press ALT or F10 to select menus                          │ Disk Editor
```

## COMMAND.COM

Everybody knows the taste of Coke, but nobody knows the secret formula. A perfume company will give you a whiff of the latest scent, but never a hint of its mysterious ingredients. If you look at your DOS directory, you'll see all the files that make up the operating system, but you won't see how it works. The secret that makes DOS what it is lies within a file called COMMAND.COM. This file is the command processor that carries out all of DOS's most important functions. The other programs in DOS send requests and data to COMMAND.COM, which works its magic upon them and sends them back.

DOS files are identified with a *file name* of eight characters or less followed by a period and a three-character *extension*.

C:\NEWSLETT\DEC\STORY.TXT

C:\NEWSLETT\DEC\LOGO.BMP

C:\NEWSLETT\DEC

C:\NEWSLETT\DEC\MAIN.DOC

...SLETT\DEC\MASTHEAD.DOC

You can tell a lot about a file by looking at its extension. Program files (files that contain instructions for running software) always have an .EXE, .COM, or .BAT extension. Data files often have extensions that tell you what type of file they are and which program created them. A .TXT or .DOC file, for example, is a text or document file probably created by a word processor; a .BMP file is a graphic bitmap file; and a .FON file is a file that contains information on a font.

You can view the names of files contained in a given directory with DOS's DIR command. Directory and subdirectory names are always preceded by a backslash (\). Subdirectories can reside within directories; these are referred to as *nested subdirectories*. So to see the names of files in the \SYSTEM subdirectory of the \WINDOWS directory, you would use the command DIR C:\WINDOWS\SYSTEM.

CONTINUED ON NEXT PAGE ➡

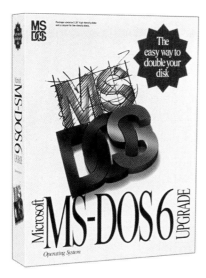

### THE DIFFERENCE A DECADE MAKES

Microsoft's DOS has come a long way since its introduction with the first IBM PC back in 1981. The original version of DOS could only store data on one side of a floppy disk. The ability to work with hard drives was added in DOS 2.0, when IBM created the PC-XT in 1983. DOS 3.0 represented a major step forward, adding many new commands and support for 80286 and 80386 microprocessors, and making it possible to use PCs in a network. With each new version, there are improvements. Today, DOS 6.0 comes with a graphical screen, clever compression programs that save disk space, and a raft of software tools that approach the power of commercial programs. Yet, at its heart, DOS maintains the same purpose and character that it had a decade ago: the organizing force behind modern PCs.

### COMMANDING THE MACHINE

DOS comes with a variety of commands for operating the computer's drives and other hardware, managing memory, and manipulating files and directories. There are dozens of DOS commands—you can find out more about them by reading your DOS manual, or if you're using DOS version 5 or later (type VER at the C:\> prompt to find out), you can type HELP at the prompt for a listing of DOS commands. The order and punctuation used to issue a command is referred to as its *syntax;* a complete command is called a *command string.* You might issue a typical command—say, if you wanted to copy all the Windows wallpaper (.BMP) files to a floppy disk in drive B:—as shown here.

Source file, which is the file(s) DOS will copy

Command prompt    Command    Path of source file(s)

C:\> COPY C:\W

## AUTOEXEC.BAT

This file, which is usually located in the root directory of the C: drive, is the second place your computer looks for instructions when you turn it on. (The first place it looks is in the floppy drive—a safeguard in DOS that lets you start, or *boot*, your computer even if your hard disk is damaged.) Your PC reads through the AUTOEXEC.BAT file line by line, following the instructions as it goes. Your computer's AUTOEXEC.BAT file may not contain all these lines, and it may include others that aren't here. This is just an example.

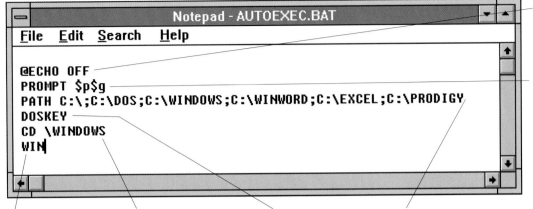

```
Notepad - AUTOEXEC.BAT
File   Edit   Search   Help

@ECHO OFF
PROMPT $p$g
PATH C:\;C:\DOS;C:\WINDOWS;C:\WINWORD;C:\EXCEL;C:\PRODIGY
DOSKEY
CD \WINDOWS
WIN
```

The @ECHO OFF command tells DOS not to display the commands in the AUTOEXEC.BAT file as it executes them.

PROMPT $p$g tells DOS the format of the *prompt* you want it to display when it's ready to accept a command. The $p causes the prompt to show the drive and directory DOS is currently in, and the $g displays a greater-than sign (>) to separate the prompt from any commands you may enter. So PROMPT $p$g will display C:\WINDOWS> if \WINDOWS is the current directory.

WIN tells DOS to start up the Windows environment.

CD \WINDOWS forces DOS to go to the \WINDOWS directory. CD (change directory) is a very handy command for moving around among your disk's files and directories.

DOSKEY tells DOS to run the DOSKEY program. To find DOSKEY.COM, the file that will execute the program, the operating system looks through the path and finds the directories on file in the DOS directory.

This line is the AUTOEXEC.BAT file's *path statement*, which tells DOS which directories to look in whenever you issue a command that can't be run from the current directory.

Destination disk for copied files (in this case, a floppy disk in drive B:)

The wildcard character * designates all files in a given group (in this case, all files with a .BMP extension in the C:\WINDOWS directory).

A switch that causes the COPY command to verify that the new files were written correctly; switches are options that can be specified for DOS commands

```
DOWS\*.BMP B:/v
```

PY C:\

A PC's operating system is a lot like a toolbox you use at home: You start by doing simple chores with a few essentials—hammer, screwdriver, pliers. Over time, as particular problems came up, you can use more specialized tools—hacksaws, routers, drills. Eventually, you'll be able to take advantage of a wide variety of gadgets, each designed for a specific task. The same thing happens as you continue to work with a PC's operating system: You begin with the essentials—commands for formatting disks, creating directories, copying files, and so on—but, over time, you discover problems that can no longer be solved with those commands. So you take advantage of interesting, specialized software tools that can be helpful if used properly, but confusing or even dangerous if you don't understand them. DOS comes with its own set of special-use tools, called utilities. If you learn how to use them, they can make your personal computing experience much richer. Here are a few of the most interesting programs in the DOS toolkit.

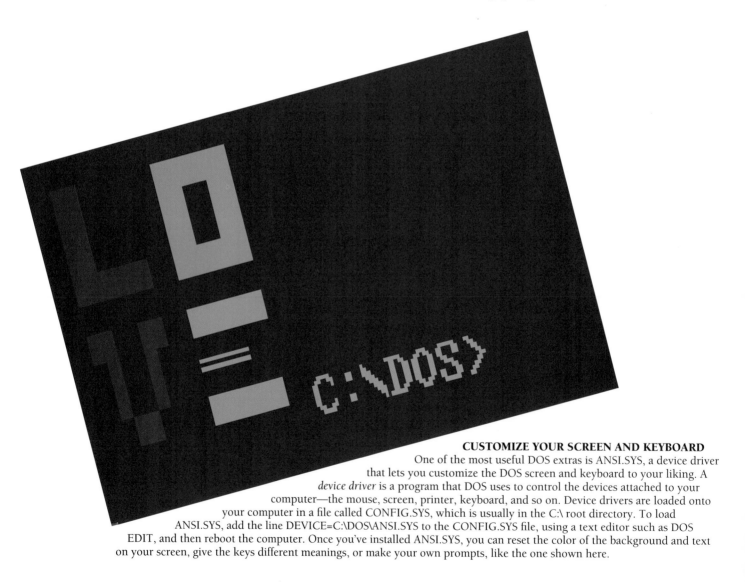

**CUSTOMIZE YOUR SCREEN AND KEYBOARD**
One of the most useful DOS extras is ANSI.SYS, a device driver that lets you customize the DOS screen and keyboard to your liking. A *device driver* is a program that DOS uses to control the devices attached to your computer—the mouse, screen, printer, keyboard, and so on. Device drivers are loaded onto your computer in a file called CONFIG.SYS, which is usually in the C:\ root directory. To load ANSI.SYS, add the line DEVICE=C:\DOS\ANSI.SYS to the CONFIG.SYS file, using a text editor such as DOS EDIT, and then reboot the computer. Once you've installed ANSI.SYS, you can reset the color of the background and text on your screen, give the keys different meanings, or make your own prompts, like the one shown here.

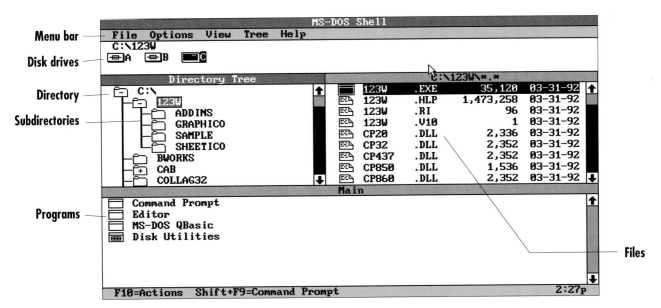

**Menu bar** — MS-DOS Shell
File  Options  View  Tree  Help

C:\123W

**Disk drives** — ⊟A  ⊟B  ⊟C

**Directory** — Directory Tree                          C:\123W\*.*

**Subdirectories** —
┌─ C:\
│  └─ 123W
│     ├─ ADDINS
│     ├─ GRAPHICO
│     ├─ SAMPLE
│     └─ SHEETICO
├─ BWORKS
├─ CAB
└─ COLLAG32

| 123W | .EXE | 35,120 | 03-31-92 |
| 123W | .HLP | 1,473,258 | 03-31-92 |
| 123W | .RI | 96 | 03-31-92 |
| 123W | .V10 | 1 | 03-31-92 |
| CP20 | .DLL | 2,336 | 03-31-92 |
| CP32 | .DLL | 2,352 | 03-31-92 |
| CP437 | .DLL | 2,352 | 03-31-92 |
| CP850 | .DLL | 1,536 | 03-31-92 |
| CP860 | .DLL | 2,352 | 03-31-92 |

Main

**Programs** —
☐ Command Prompt
☐ Editor
☐ MS-DOS QBasic
☐ Disk Utilities

**Files**

F10=Actions  Shift+F9=Command Prompt                    2:27p

## THE DOS SHELL

If you type DOSSHELL at the prompt in DOS version 4.0 or later, you'll start the DOS Shell program, which gives you a visual overview of the files and directories on your PC. The shell has tools for searching through all the files on a disk; creating and deleting directories; copying, deleting, and moving files; and running programs. There's nothing you can do with the Shell that you can't do with typed commands using plain old DOS, but because you pick the commands from menus using a mouse, there's not so much to remember. (If you don't have a mouse, you can use the Alt key to activate the menus, the cursor and tab keys to move around in them, and the Enter key to make selections.)

### THE DOS EDITOR

DOS 5.0 and later versions come with their own word processor for making and editing text documents. If you type EDIT at the command prompt, you'll get a screen with four menus at the top. To see what's on the menus, either click on them with the mouse, or press the Alt key and use the cursor keys to move through them. Click the mouse or press the Enter key to make selections. A word processor like this one makes it easy to copy and paste text or to search through files for certain words or phrases.

File  **Edit**  Search  Options                          Help
                                    ┌─ DOSHELP.HLP ─┐
CHKDSK   │ Cut        Shift+Del │ lays a status report.
CLS      │ Copy       Ctrl+Ins  │
COMMAN   │ Paste      Shift+Ins │ of the MS-DOS command interpreter.
COMP     │ Clear      Del       │ of two files or sets of files.
COPY     └──────────────────────┘ les to another location.
CTTY       Changes the terminal device used to control your system.
DATE       Displays or sets the date.
DEBUG      Runs Debug, a program testing and editing tool.
DEL        Deletes one or more files.
DIR        Displays a list of files and subdirectories in a directory.
DISKCOMP   Compares the contents of two floppy disks.
DISKCOPY   Copies the contents of one floppy disk to another.
DOSKEY     Edits command lines, recalls MS-DOS commands, and creates macros.
DOSSHELL   Starts MS-DOS Shell.
ECHO       Displays messages, or turns command echoing on or off.
EDIT       Starts MS-DOS Editor, which creates and changes ASCII files.
EDLIN      Starts Edlin, a line-oriented text editor.
EMM386     Turns on or off EMM386 expanded memory support.
ERASE      Deletes one or more files.
EXE2BIN    Converts .EXE (executable) files to binary format.
EXIT       Quits the COMMAND.COM program (command interpreter).

F1=Help │ Deletes selected text and copies it to buffer      00038:001

### DOSKEY

It can be difficult to type in complicated commands (such as the ones you use to design your own prompts) over and over again. That's when the DOSKEY command stacker comes in handy. DOSKEY lets you view and edit the commands you've typed by keeping them in a command stack (known generically as a *buffer*, a holding area that offers temporary storage for data). DOSKEY comes with MS-DOS version 5.0 and later. Once you type DOSKEY at the prompt (or put it in your AUTOEXEC.BAT file—see the previous chapter), it waits in the background for you to send it a command. See the box at right for some of the keys you can use with the DOSKEY stacker.

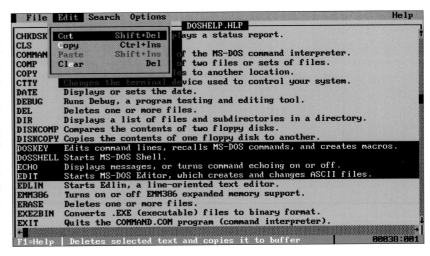

C:\> DIR A: *.*

C:\> COPY A: *.* C:\LETTERS

C:\> CD \LETTERS

C:\LETTERS > DIR

C:\LETTERS > DEL A: *.*

**Keys and Results**

| Up arrow | Recalls the previous command; works backward through the command stack |
| Down arrow | Recalls the command after the one currently displayed; works forward through the stack |
| Page Up | Recalls the oldest command in the buffer |
| Page Down | Recalls the newest command in the buffer |
| F7 | Displays the entire command stack |
| F8 | Searches for old commands |

# Do This First!
# Make an Emergency Disk

*NOTE: This project assumes that you're using MS-DOS 5 or a later version.*
Before you explore DOS's commands, files, and directories, it's wise to make an emergency disk to help you recover from mishaps. If your computer's hard disk ever fails for some reason, or if your hard disk's AUTOEXEC.BAT file becomes unusable, a floppy disk can start up the machine and give you the tools you need to determine what's wrong. Follow these steps to make an emergency floppy:

1. Turn on the PC and go to the DOS prompt (usually it looks like C:\> or something similar).

2. Type A: at the prompt and hit Enter. The prompt should now look something like this:

   ```
   A:\>
   ```

3. Insert a spare floppy disk into the computer's A: drive. (If your PC has both a 5 ¼-inch and a 3 ½-inch drive, chances are the A: drive is the 5 ¼-inch one.)

4. Type **FORMAT A: /S** at the prompt. What you see on your screen should look like this:

   ```
   A:\>FORMAT A: /S
   ```

   Then hit the Enter key. The FORMAT command organizes the disk into tracks and sectors. The /S switch copies the system files (including COMMAND.COM, DOS's command processor) to the disk so it can start the machine.

5. Copy your AUTOEXEC.BAT and CONFIG.SYS files from your hard disk to the emergency floppy. These files are probably in the root directory of the C: drive. If so, the commands would be

   ```
   COPY C:\AUTOEXEC.BAT A:
   COPY C:\CONFIG.SYS A:
   ```

6. At the prompt, type

   ```
   TYPE C:\AUTOEXEC.BAT
   ```

   The contents of the AUTOEXEC.BAT file appear on the screen. Make a note of any batch files (files with a .BAT extension) that are in AUTOEXEC.BAT, and copy them to the floppy disk as well. Then start the DOS Editor, open the AUTOEXEC.BAT file, and change the path to any batch files you've copied so the machine will look for them on the A: drive.

7. At the prompt, type

   ```
   TYPE C:\CONFIG.SYS
   ```

   The lines in the file that start with DEVICE or DEVICEHIGH are lines that load device drivers, which are software programs that tell the PC how to operate certain devices or memory managers. Drivers often have .SYS extensions. Make a note of the drivers included in the CONFIG.SYS file and copy them to the floppy disk, too. Also, change the references to these files from their hard-disk location to A:.

8. Finally, copy the DOS Editor and QBASIC to the floppy with the following lines:

   ```
   COPY C:\DOS\EDIT.COM A:
   COPY C:\DOS\QBASIC.EXE A:
   ```

   Check to be sure the emergency disk works properly by trying to boot from it. After you're sure that it starts the machine and other devices properly, clearly label the disk EMERGENCY DISK, and keep it handy.

# Do-It-Yourself Prompts

You can create an endless variety of DOS prompts by loading the ANSI.SYS driver in your CONFIG.SYS file. See "Customize Your Screen and Keyboard" in the "DOS Utilities" chapter for information on how to load ANSI.SYS onto your PC.

When designing your own prompts, you use ANSI *metastrings,* small pieces of code that tell ANSI what to display on your screen. To display your prompt, type

```
PROMPT
```

followed by the words or graphics you want to use in your prompt. Do not press the Enter key until the end of the prompt.

If you devise a prompt you like and want to use it whenever you use DOS, just put the new PROMPT command in your AUTO-EXEC.BAT file.

The strings for setting the colors in your prompt look like this:

```
$e[xx;xx;...m
```

where *xx* is the number for the color attribute, semicolons separate each number, and the metastring ends with an *m*. (NOTE: ANSI.SYS is case sensitive, meaning that you must type lowercase and capital letters as shown.) Here are some of the color attributes that ANSI can control:

| Color | Foreground | Background |
|-------|-----------|------------|
| Black | 30 | 40 |
| Red | 31 | 41 |
| Green | 32 | 42 |
| Yellow | 33 | 43 |
| Blue | 34 | 44 |
| Magenta | 35 | 45 |
| Cyan | 36 | 46 |
| White | 37 | 47 |

Here are other metastrings you might want to use:

| What you enter | What appears |
|----------------|--------------|
| $t | Current time |
| $d | Current date |
| $p | Current drive and path |
| $_ | Moves cursor to the next line (underline character) |
| $e[cC | Moves the cursor to the right *c* columns |

And here are some graphics characters that will come in handy. To include these in your prompt, hold down the Alt key and then type the character's number *using the numeric keypad.*

| Character | Alt-key number | Character | Alt-key number |
|-----------|----------------|-----------|----------------|
| ■ | 223 | = | 205 |
| ■ | 220 | ╗ | 187 |
| ▌ | 221 | ╔ | 201 |
| ▐ | 222 | ╚ | 200 |
| █ | 219 | ╝ | 188 |
| │ | 179 | ║ | 186 |

To get you started, here's the metastring for the prompt on page 30. Remember to put all the characters on a continuous line—don't press Enter until you come to the very end of the prompt. And wherever you see a number sign in these prompts, type a *space*.

```
PROMPT=$e[44;31m$_#■###$e[32m■■■$
_#$e[31m■■■#$e[32m■■■$_#$e[35m■#
■#$e[36m■■■$_#$e[35m##■#$e[36m==$
_##$e[35m■##$e[36m■■■#$p$g
```

And here's a prompt of Bart Simpson:

```
PROMPT=$e[1;33m|\/\/\/|$_|$e[6C|$_|
###$e[36m0#0$e[1;33m)$_C$e[6C_)$_#|
#$e[;31m,___$e[1;33m|#Command#me,#
dude!$_#|#|###/#$e[m#
```

# Windows Basics

You learn specific facts best through words but learn unfamiliar concepts and ideas best through pictures. If you wanted to communicate with a creature from another planet, you'd draw pictures. Nowhere is this basic rule of communication more true than in computing. Most of what computers do is unfamiliar to us. Unfortunately, getting a computer to create pictures is much harder than getting it to print words. Not until recently—only in the past few years—have IBM-compatible PCs offered a graphical picture-based way to compute. (Apple Computers have used a graphical interface since the early 1980s.) Microsoft Windows is the most popular form of graphical computing today. Windows is a software program that puts a graphical face over DOS and makes PCs much easier to use.

## PROGRAM MANAGER

A computer that shows you what you can do with it is easier to use. That's what the Windows Program Manager does—it shows you the programs you can run in the form of buttonlike pictures called *icons*, and it lets you organize all your programs on the screen any way you want. Instead of typing in long DOS commands, you can accomplish tasks in Windows—such as copying a file or starting a program—by using the mouse to select choices from menus or to click on icons. That's why Windows is called a *graphical user interface*, or GUI: It puts a visual graphical shell around bare-bones DOS. Instead of files and directories, Windows has *program items* and *program groups*—each icon in a window represents a program item, and each window represents a group.

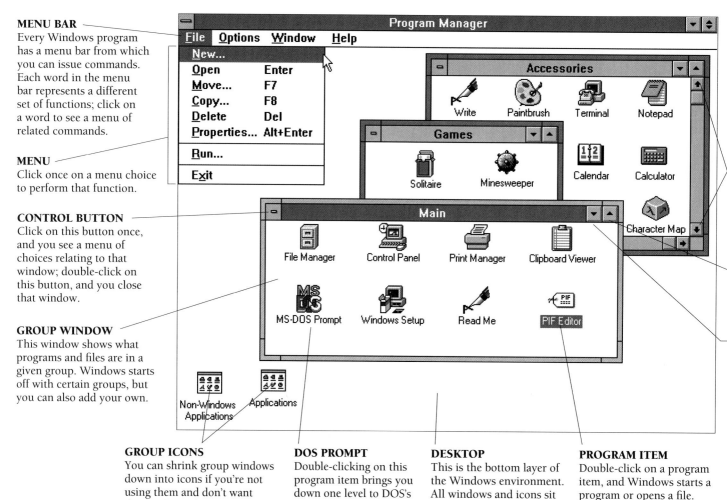

**MENU BAR**
Every Windows program has a menu bar from which you can issue commands. Each word in the menu bar represents a different set of functions; click on a word to see a menu of related commands.

**MENU**
Click once on a menu choice to perform that function.

**CONTROL BUTTON**
Click on this button once, and you see a menu of choices relating to that window; double-click on this button, and you close that window.

**GROUP WINDOW**
This window shows what programs and files are in a given group. Windows starts off with certain groups, but you can also add your own.

**GROUP ICONS**
You can shrink group windows down into icons if you're not using them and don't want them to be in the way.

**DOS PROMPT**
Double-clicking on this program item brings you down one level to DOS's C:\> prompt.

**DESKTOP**
This is the bottom layer of the Windows environment. All windows and icons sit on the desktop.

**PROGRAM ITEM**
Double-click on a program item, and Windows starts a program or opens a file.

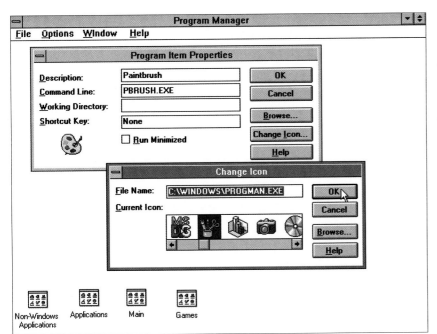

## HOW TO CHANGE AN ICON

One way to change the look of your desktop is to customize the icons you use for your files and programs. To do this, first highlight the icon you want to change by clicking on it once. Then go to the File menu and select Properties. A dialog box called Program Item Properties appears. Click on the Change Icon button, and another dialog box appears. Choose another icon from the selection, or fill in a file name other than the one that goes with the program item. Two file names to try are C:\WINDOWS\PROGMAN.EXE and if you're using Windows 3.1, C:\WINDOWS\MORICONS.DLL. Once you've found the icon you want, click on OK twice (once in each dialog box), and—voilà!—a new icon appears with that program item.

## CUSTOMIZE YOUR DESKTOP

Windows gives you lots of tools for making your screen workspace look just the way you like it. The Control Panel is the first place to go if you want to experiment with different colors and patterns on your Windows desktop. Open the Control Panel by double-clicking on the Control Panel icon (it's in the Main group). You'll find another group of icons in the Control Panel window; explore the Color and the Desktop settings. When you've settled on a desktop you like, click on the OK button in the top right corner.

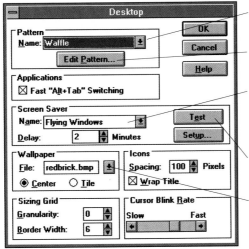

Click on this arrow to see a selection of patterns you can add to a solid-color desktop.

You can edit the desktop pattern or create your own by clicking on this button.

*A screen saver* is a program that automatically covers the screen with an animated pattern when you're not working at the computer. Click on this arrow to see the screen saver choices.

For a demonstration of the selected screen saver, click on this button.

Choose from a selection of predefined *wallpapers*—the backgrounds beneath windows, icons, and dialog boxes—by clicking on this arrow.

**SCROLL BAR**
Click on the arrows or drag the little box to move around in a document or group window.

**MAXIMIZE BUTTON**
Click on this button to open up the window so it covers the entire screen.

**MINIMIZE BUTTON**
Click on this button to shrink a group window or program item into an icon.

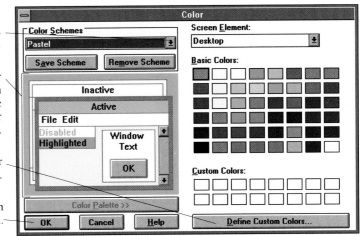

Click on this arrow to view a menu of predefined color schemes.

This is a replica of your Windows desktop. Click on an area where you want to change the color, and select a color from the grid at the right.

Click on this button to define your own custom colors for the screen.

Once you've settled on a combination of colors you like, click on this button.

All Windows programs share certain visual tools. If you look at the screens on these two pages, you'll see that all the screens have menu bars; title bars; maximize, minimize, and control buttons; and many other features that you saw in the Program Manager described on the previous page. This makes trying new programs much easier—you can explore your computer with confidence, since you already know a lot about how each program works. The programs you see on these pages are part of a handy set of small applications built into Windows. They're all in the Accessories program group that Windows creates when you first install it on your PC.

**PAINTBRUSH**

Paintbrush is a handy drawing and painting program tool for creating your own pictures. Experiment with the drawing and erasing tools on the left side of the screen. Express yourself with the colors from the palette at the bottom of the screen. Select Zoom In from the View menu and click on an area of your drawing to get a pixel-by-pixel—that is, dot-by-dot—closeup. For instructions on how to make your masterpiece into Windows wallpaper, see the projects on the next page.

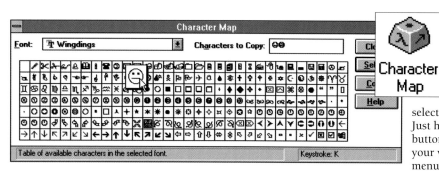

**CHARACTER MAP**

If you have Windows 3.1 or later, you'll see the Character Map icon in your Accessories group. Windows gives you a lot more characters and symbols to choose from than those on your keyboard. If you're working in Write or any other word processor, you can open the Character Map, select any character, and paste it into your document. Just highlight the character you want, click on the Select button, and click on the Copy button. Then go back to your word processor and choose Paste from the Edit menu—the character appears wherever the cursor is.

**CLOCK**

The Windows Clock is straightforward. From the Settings menu, you can choose either a digital or traditional clock face, size the clock to take up an area ranging from the size of a postage stamp to the entire screen, change the font of the digital display, and make other adjustments. And here's a trick: If you want the clock in Windows 3.1 to always be in view, click once on the Clock's Control button (the gray square in the upper left-hand corner) and check the Always on Top option.

### WRITE

The Write program is a word processor that you can use to create and edit documents. You can change indentation, paragraph spacing, and letter type, size, and style. Find out how by typing in some text, selecting it (by holding down the left mouse button and dragging the cursor so the text appears white on black), and trying the various Character and Paragraph menu options.

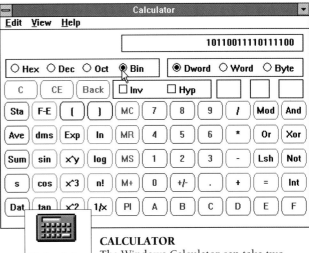

### CALCULATOR

The Windows Calculator can take two forms. The Standard view gives you all the functions of an ordinary desktop calculator: You can use it to add, subtract, multiply, divide, and calculate square roots and percentages. The Scientific view offers statistical and trigonometric functions and lets you choose from a variety of number systems, including binary. Type in a regular decimal number and then click the Bin button to see the number's binary equivalent.

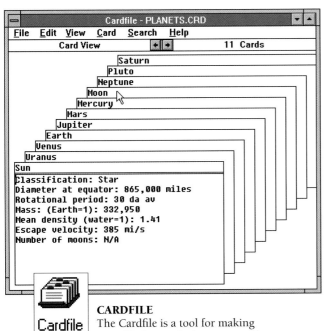

### CARDFILE

The Cardfile is a tool for making sets of index cards that are sorted automatically. You can use the cards to store names, addresses, phone numbers, notes, or any other information you want to file by keywords. You can save separate stacks of cards in different files.

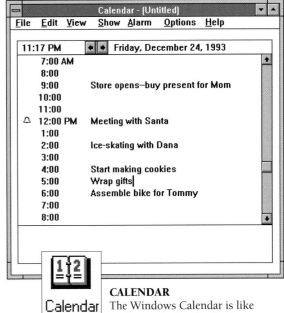

### CALENDAR

The Windows Calendar is like an electronic date book. You can schedule baseball practice or homework assignments, set the alarm to notify you of an upcoming TV show, or see what day your birthday falls on next year.

# Make Your Own Windows Wallpaper

As you saw in "Windows Basics," the Windows Desktop dialog box makes it easy to decorate your Windows screen with wallpaper, patterns, colors, and other special effects. Windows comes with a variety of ready-to-use wallpapers to dress up your screen, but making your own can be even more fun. Try different wallpapers for holidays, birthdays, and other special events. Or create a set of wallpapers to suit your moods. Here's how you do it.

1. Start by opening Paintbrush (it's in the Accessories group).

2. Choose the size of your drawing. Decide whether you want your wallpaper to be one big picture that takes up the whole screen, or lots of little pictures that repeat in a pattern across the screen. Once you've decided, select Options, Image Attributes and set the measurements for the image you're going to draw. On a typical PC screen with VGA graphics, an image measuring 6.5 inches wide by 5 inches high will fill up the entire screen.

3. Start drawing. Be sure to save your work (File, Save) after you've drawn something you want to keep. You may want to start with an outline (which you should save), and then fill in the various spaces using the paint-roller tool.

4. When you've put the finishing touches on your creation, save it by selecting File, Save. Give it a .BMP extension, and save it in the \WINDOWS subdirectory.

5. To apply your wallpaper to your desktop, go into the Control Panel (it's in the Main group) and select Desktop. In the dialog box that appears, you'll see a Wallpaper section. Click on the arrow to see a drop-down list of the files you can choose from to make wallpaper. Select the file you just made in Paintbrush, and check whether you want to center it or "tile" it (that is, have it repeat in a pattern). Click on OK in the upper-right corner of the Desktop dialog box. Voilà: your own Windows wallpaper!

# Do-It-Yourself "Bar Codes"

Computers can do amazing things with typefaces, especially with the capabilities of Windows. If you have Windows 3.*x*, Microsoft Word 2.*x*, and a printer, you can use Windows Write to create neat effects with type. This project explains how to make "bar codes" that you can read if you know the trick. Here's how.

1. Open Windows Write—it's in the Accessories group.

2. Select Edit, Insert Object, and choose MS WordArt from the list.

3. To make your own "bar code," type a short, one-line message in all capital letters to replace the "Your Text Here" message in the WordArt text box. Select Best Fit for the type size, and check the Stretch Vertical box under Options. The words you typed will appear very tall and skinny in the Preview box, looking somewhat like a bar code. You may want to try different fonts—Ellensburg, Inglewood, and Marysville work especially well for

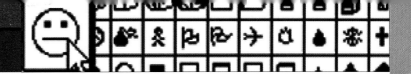

this project. Click on OK to put the stretched text into your Write document.

4. Print the document and try to read the message by tilting the paper flat and reading it horizontally. If it's still difficult to read, or if it's too easy to read without tilting it, select the text in the Write document and choose Edit, Size Picture. Move the mouse horizontally to where you want the text to reach and click on the mouse button. Experiment until you reach a good size—then print it out and see if your friends can read the message! Here's an example of how the text should look—see if you can read this message:

# Create an Address Book

Windows Cardfile is perfect for making an electronic address and phone book. If your PC is hooked up to a modem, you can even use it to dial the phone! Here's how to do it.

1. Start Cardfile—it's in the Windows Accessories group. When it first comes up, you'll see a blank card.

2. To make your first card, double-click on the top part of the card. A box titled "Index Line" pops up; fill in the name and phone number there. Start with the last name if you want the cards to be alphabetized by last name; start with the first name if you want to be able to look them up by first name. After the name, type a space and add the phone number. Include a 1 and the area code if you have a modem and you want to use your address book to directly dial long-distance numbers. Once the top line has all the information you want, click on OK. (To change the top line of a completed card, click on it once to bring it to the front of the stack, then double-click on the top line to bring up the Index Line box again and change the line.)

3. You can type in additional information, such as address, birthday, favorite color—anything that can fit on the card—in the space below the index line.

4. To add more cards, select Card, Add and repeat steps 2 and 3. As you continue to add cards, they will be arranged alphabetically. Don't forget to save the file as you work! Select File, Save and name the file.

5. To automatically dial the phone number on the top of the card, bring that card to the front of the stack and hit the F5 function key or select Card, Autodial from the menu. To set up the modem for use with all the cards in the stack (you need to do this only once), click on the Setup button and fill in the correct dial type, COM port, and baud rate.

6. To print the address book, select File, Print All. Normally, Cardfile will fit only three cards on a page. To fit more cards on a page, select File, Page Setup, delete the codes in the Header and Footer boxes, and make the margins smaller—0.5 inches or so.

# Programming

The process of writing instructions to comman a computer is called *programming*. Early comp were programmed by changing wires and flipp switches. Modern programming is done with languages that the computer translates into an electronic form it can understand (through a program called a *compiler*). The key to programming is logic, a step-by-step process of small decisions leading to a particula goal. Programming a computer is less like writing music than like developing the recipe for a complicated dinner. Each ingredient must be identified and then used in just the right amount, in just the right pot, in just the right order. Do it any other way, and the meal will fail. With a program, each piece of information, every task the computer must perform, and every resource the computer will use must be identified and used appropriately at just the right time. That makes programming one of the most difficult, detailed-oriented tasks in computing.

## A GOING-TO-SCHOOL PROGRAM

Programmers need a way to represent the basic flow of information and ideas through their software; this is most often done using a program map called a flowchart. In a flowchart, boxes of different shapes representing different operations within the program are connected by lines representing the flow of information. The flowchart shown here is a map of a program that you might use for getting to school in the morning. Like a good story, every program has a beginning and an end, which are designated here with parallelograms. Every program includes *commands*—directions that the computer must follow to achieve desired results. In this diagram, commands are shown in the rectangular boxes. A program can also distinguish whether certain conditions are true or false—as shown by the diamond-shaped part of the diagram—and execute different commands in each case. And it can take different actions depending on which of several conditions is true, as indicated by the hexagons on the flowchart.

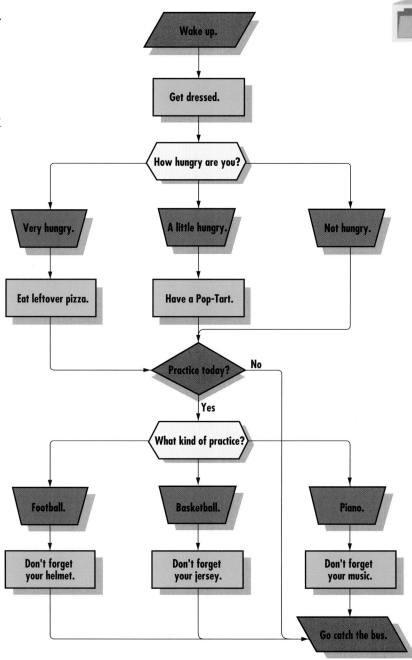

**Operating system**  **Operating environment**

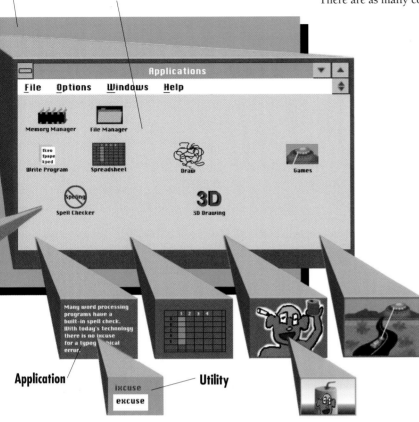

Applications

File   Options   Windows   Help

Memory Manager   File Manager   Write Program   Spreadsheet   Draw   Games

Spell Checker   3D   3D Drawing

**Application**   **Utility**

Many word processing programs have a built-in spell check. With today's technology there is no ixcuse for a typog ...hical error.

ixcuse excuse

## VARIETIES OF SOFTWARE

There are as many computer programs as there are computers, but all PC programs fall into four basic categories: operating systems, operating environments, applications, and utilities. The *operating system* is the program that reads in and supervises all other programs run by the PC. DOS, OS/2, UNIX, and Apple's System 7 are all operating systems. In addition to the operating system, your PC may have an *operating environment*—a shell that encases the operating system in a friendlier, easier-to-use wrapping. Windows, GeoWorks, and NewWave are a few examples of operating environments for IBM-compatible PCs. The third kind of program is *applications*—software designed to perform specific tasks. Word processors, spreadsheets, databases, and games are all examples of applications. Finally, there are *utilities*—small programs that provide a helping hand when used in conjunction with other software. A spelling checker for a word processor, a graphing

## WHAT'S A COMPUTER VIRUS?

A virus is a menacing program that can attach itself to files and spread to thousands of PCs in a matter of days, through infected disks or over telephone lines. The damage a virus can do may be annoying (such as displaying a message on the screen, or it may be truly destructive (such as erasing important files). Antivirus programs are designed especially to protect your PC by scanning your floppies and hard disks for common viruses.

## A TEXTILE REVOLUTION

During the late eighteenth and early nineteenth centuries, weavers required helpers, called drawboys, to lift the proper set of strings on each pass of the loom shuttle to produce a desired design. It was a painstaking task until French mechanic and builder Joseph-Marie Jacquard devised a system that automated the process with a chain of punched cards. Each card in the chain had holes that showed the pattern of threads to be lifted during one pass of the shuttle; when the entire chain had passed through the loom, one cycle in the cloth pattern was complete. What does this have to do with computers? In a way, Jacquard's stack of punched cards was the first program. His invention proved that information could be stored on a card in the form of holes (the presence of a hole meant one thing; the absence meant the opposite) and that a simple two-element system could be translated into an infinite variety of patterns. The cloth shown here is a vivid illustration of this: It is a portrait of Jacquard, woven in black and white silk, based on a program of 10,000 punched cards.

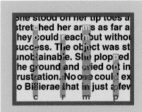

**Falling-letters virus**

**Friday the 13th virus**

**Tequila virus**

# Programming Languages

No computer language has yet been invented that allows us to simply write what we want and have the computer understand us. People use letters, numbers, mouse clicks, and other familiar symbols and actions to describe what they want a computer to do, but computers need to get their instructions in the form of electronic pulses. The translation between our instructions and the computer's response is accomplished by computer languages. Some computer languages look a lot like English—they translate words and punctuation into computer signals. Other languages look like algebra—they use numbers, equations, and other mathematical forms to describe the computer's instructions. Although all computer languages are made up of the same symbols that humans use to communicate, computer languages are really quite different because they must describe things in the most natural way for a computer to follow. That's why learning to use a computer takes so much work and practice.

### LANGUAGES AREN'T JUST FOR PEOPLE

Computer languages are like a mix of human language and math: The terms have to be very precise (as in math), but the machine can "understand" a wide variety of commands and statements, as long as they're phrased in the correct way (as in human language). Because a computer recognizes only language that it's been programmed to recognize, you have to be very exact when writing a computer program. The particular way you must phrase a command is called the *command syntax*. Human languages have rules of syntax, too—also known as grammar—but you're probably not consciously aware of the rules because your language is "programmed" into your brain at a very young age.

Both computer languages and human languages don't have any meaning by themselves—we have to give them meaning through a shared understanding of which words stand for which ideas or objects. If you try to communicate with someone who doesn't speak your language, you need an interpreter—someone who translates the meanings back and forth between one language and another. The computer needs an interpreter, too—a program that translates programming code into electronic impulses the computer can understand.

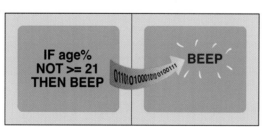

Another feature computer languages have in common with human languages is that they develop dialects—local variations that are used to adapt the language to particular environments. In human languages, the variations are generally regional and take the form of accents and small differences in vocabulary. In computer languages, adaptations and improvements are made so the same language can be understood by different machines and operating systems.

## THE MEN BEHIND THE LANGUAGE

The BASIC programming language has been around for almost thirty years and it's still going strong, with many variations still in use. Originally, BASIC was developed at Dartmouth College by professors John Kemeny (left) and Thomas Kurtz (right). They wanted to develop a language that could be used by people with little or no computer experience. Clearly they succeeded: As microcomputers became popular at the end of the 1970s and into the 1980s, BASIC became the programming language of the personal computer revolution.

## BASIC VOCABULARY

BASIC (Beginner's All-purpose Symbolic Instruction Code) is one of the easiest PC languages to learn and use. Its English-like instructions and statements can perform a variety of tasks, from drawing to making sounds to asking for and acting on user input. Here are a few of the commands, statements, operators, and variable types (like the verbs, nouns, and other parts of speech in the English language) you'll find in QBASIC, the variety of BASIC that's included with DOS 5 and later. (Note: Italic phrases represent user-defined variables.)

| Expression | Meaning |
|---|---|
| CLS | Clears the user's screen |
| PRINT *"string"* | Displays the *string* on the screen (the string can be almost any word or set of words) |
| *variable*$ | Designates a string variable |
| *variable*% | Designates a number variable |
| + | Add |
| − | Subtract |
| * | Multiply |
| / | Divide |
| = | Is equal to |
| <> | Is not equal to |
| > | Is greater than |
| < | Is less than |
| IF *condition* THEN *statement* ELSE *statement* | Specifies an action to be taken if the *condition* is met or not met |
| INPUT *variable* | Asks the user for a response and stores it in a variable |

## MANY LANGUAGES TO DO THE SAME JOB

Below are programs written in four languages. Each program instructs the computer to display the following lines on the screen:

```
TEST
1
2
3
4
5
6
7
8
9
10
DONE
```

As you can see, some of the languages are more like English, and some are more like math. Note the vocabulary of the different languages. For example, each language uses a different command to tell the computer to write something on the screen: In BASIC it's PRINT, in Pascal it's WriteLn, in C++ it's <<, and in xBase it's ?.

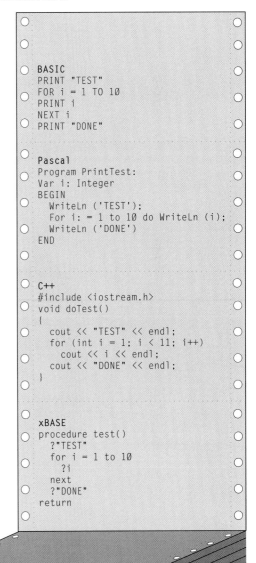

```
BASIC
PRINT "TEST"
FOR i = 1 TO 10
PRINT i
NEXT i
PRINT "DONE"


Pascal
Program PrintTest:
Var i: Integer
BEGIN
    WriteLn ('TEST');
    For i: = 1 to 10 do WriteLn (i);
    WriteLn ('DONE')
END


C++
#include <iostream.h>
void doTest()
{
    cout << "TEST" << endl;
    for (int i = 1; i < 11; i++)
        cout << i << endl;
    cout << "DONE" << endl;
}


xBASE
procedure test()
    ?"TEST"
    for i = 1 to 10
      ?i
    next
    ?"DONE"
return
```

# Games, Sound, and Graphics

Computers make great game machines because when you play a game with them, they can play right back. Unlike TVs, computers don't just show you a game, they interact with you. Until recently, the ability of computers to entertain was limited by poor graphics and sound—your TV looked a lot better than your computer screen, and your stereo produced many more interesting sounds. But with the excellent graphics of today's PCs and the emergence of stereo PC sound, computers are becoming marvelous devices for entertainment of all kinds. Already we're seeing entertainment systems that combine the characteristics of PCs with the roles of stereo, TV, radio, and VCR, blurring the line between computers and television. Because they will be interactive, future PCs will let you be your own radio deejay, a contestant in the game shows you watch, or the cameraperson on the movies you request. In this multimedia future, computing and entertainment will be the same thing.

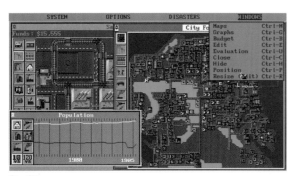

SimCity

Where in Space Is Carmen Sandiego?

World Circuit

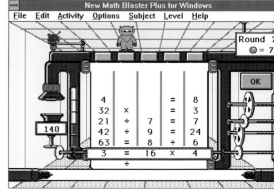

New Math Blaster Plus

## A GAME-PLAYER'S DELIGHT

No other kind of software has benefited more from the creativity and imagination of programmers than games have. Ever since the very first graphical computer game, called Pong, software designers have been improving on the computer's ability to dazzle the eye, test the reflexes, and challenge the mind. Some games are *simulations*—elaborate scenarios that put you in command of an F-15 fighter, make you the mayor of a big city, or seat you behind the wheel of a race car. Others, such as Where in Space Is Carmen Sandiego? and New Math Blaster Plus, help you learn while you play. Other categories include sports, role-playing (in which you take the part of an imaginary character and try to reach a goal with a limited set of powers and tools), and action/adventure games. With their vivid animation and realistic sound effects, the possibilities of computer games are limited only by your imagination.

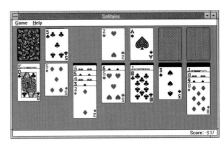

## CHESS: THE ULTIMATE COMPUTER GAME

With its logical rules and think-ahead strategy, chess has always been a natural for computers. The first chess program,written in 1957, was designed to select the seven best moves it could make, the seven best replies to each of those moves, and the seven best replies to each reply. That pales in comparison with today's best chess-playing computers. IBM's Deep Thought chess computer, for example, can analyze 800,000 chessboard positions per second. Such prowess has earned Deep Thought the equivalent of a grand master rating by the U.S. Chess Federation. The chess game shown above combines the skill of computer chess with the realistic play of regular pieces. It's not as powerful as Deep Thought, but it makes a great challenger and coach.

## NATIVE WINDOWS GAMES

If you have Windows 3.0 or later, chances are you've become addicted to Windows Solitaire, a graphical, computerized version of the single-player card game. Once you've tried it, you'll wonder how you ever played the game without dragging and clicking the cards with a mouse.

Windows 3.1 also includes a game called Minesweeper. The object is to uncover all the mines on the game board without blowing yourself up. Minesweeper is 10 percent luck and 90 percent skill; most of what it takes to master the strategy is practice.

## THE WORLD OF GRAPHICS

Personal computers have revolutionized the graphics and printing industries over the past decade. Art and design work that only a few years ago required equipment costing millions of dollars can now be done on a regular PC. With any kind of printer, you can use programs like the one shown here to make banners, invitations, greeting cards, newsletters, and more. You can also take advantage of *clip art,* collections of drawings that come on disk and can be displayed on the screen or put into documents (like the world, left, and mouth, right).

## RECORDING AND CREATING SOUND

One great enhancement you can make to improve the play of computer games is to add a sound board to your PC. Most sound boards are simple add-in cards (see the chapter, "Inside a Computer Box") containing a controller chip that converts the analog signals of sound into digital signals that the computer can process and store, and vice versa. *Analog signals* are electrical signals that vary continuously, as in a sound wave; *digital signals* are noncontinuous, going from level to level or step to step. A membrane in the microphone generates analog waves that are sent to the sound board's analog-to-digital converter (ADC), which converts the waves into the binary on-and-off signals the computer can understand. To play back a sound, the card's digital-to-analog converter (DAC) translates the digitized signals the computer is storing into an electric current that vibrates the speakers to generate the sound.

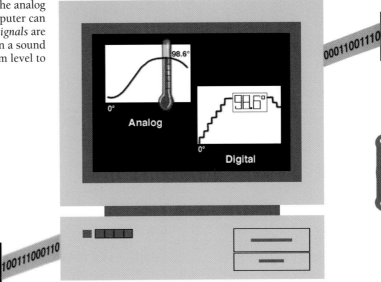

# Prodigy

Imagine being able to go to the library, the newsstand, the clubhouse where your friends hang out, the arcade, the mall, and the town square—all without ever leaving your house. That's what you can do with your PC right now through the world of electronic services. From the comfort of your desk chair, you can dial up knowledge, companionship, catalogs of things to buy—almost anything you can imagine. Plus, you can connect to thousands of other people, many of them just like you! This chapter focuses on Prodigy, an electronic service with a graphical interface.

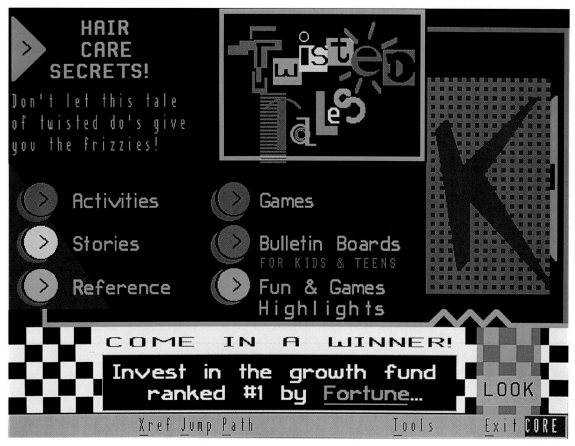

## A PLACE FOR KIDS

Prodigy is a dial-up network with lots of games and activities for kids and adults. To use it or any other electronic service, you need a *modem,* which is a device that sends computer signals over phone lines. Once you pay the monthly fee—Prodigy is a subscription service, much like a magazine—you can connect your computer to Prodigy's computer (in other words, you can "go on line") and communicate with the millions of other members on the service. The screen you see here is the Kids Highlights screen. If you press the buttons next to the selections—Activities, Stories, Reference, and so on—you'll see other menus much like this one, with selections related to that topic. What will you find there? Here's an example: In the Reference section, you'll have access to the entire *Academic American Encyclopedia,* a science column called Beyond Belief, an on-line version of the Ask Beth column, a current events feature called Background on the News, a Software Guide with product reviews, and more. The gray command bar along the bottom of the screen lets you navigate around the hundreds of other areas of the service, from travel to news to computers to politics—you can even send a message to the president! Two especially handy commands are the Menu command, which backs you up to the previous menu, and the Jump command, which lets you move from anywhere on Prodigy to anywhere else if you know the correct Jumpword.

## KEEP IN TOUCH WITH BULLETIN BOARDS

Prodigy is host to dozens of *computer bulletin boards*—on-line forums where you and other callers can post public messages and carry on "virtual conversations."

Prodigy has two separate boards for teenagers and kids under 12. To get to them, Jump: the club (if you're under 12) or Jump: teens bb (if you're 12 to 20). With hundreds of members signing on and writing messages each day, you'll find that the bulletin boards never look the same twice. Follow these guidelines for getting the most out of the time you spend on the boards.

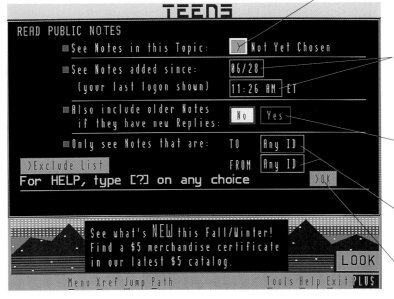

Click on this button (or move to it with the arrow keys and press Enter) to see a list of topics. Select the one you want to start with, and a list of subtopics (called *subjects* in Prodigy lingo) appears. Just choose one and start reading.

These boxes show the last date and time you were on Prodigy. To see earlier messages, go into the date box and set the date back by a week or two.

Check Yes if you visit the bulletin board often but want a reminder about how a certain *thread* (string of messages) got started.

Use these boxes if you want to see only messages to or from a certain ID.

When all your options are set, click on OK.

### THE BABY-SITTER'S CLUB

Based on the series of books about a group of friends who babysit after school and on vacations, the Baby-Sitter's Club section of Prodigy (Jump: baby-sitters club) includes stories that tell you about club-member's problems and then let you vote on the best solution. You'll also find a column with tips for real-life babysitting situations, a date reminder that will send you Prodigy mail to remind you of important dates, and an advice column by the author of the books.

### SMARTKIDS QUIZ: TEST YOUR KNOWLEDGE

SmartKids Quiz is a weekly feature that asks you questions about a certain topic, such as U.S. history or fishing. The quiz is multiple choice, with three answers to choose from for each question. Even if you don't know anything about the topic, you'll learn plenty as you work your way through the answers. You get a Certificate of Merit after going through the SmartKids Quiz, and if you're the high scorer for the week, you win the Real Genius Award.

### FOR KIDS BY KIDS

This weekly feature includes lots of great stories and ideas written by kids. Each week the For Kids By Kids section (Jump: fkbk) includes a question for you to answer and a summary of the best answers given to the previous week's question. Some sample questions: What's the yuckiest thing you ever found on the beach? What's the scariest amusement-park ride you've ever been on? What is your favorite after-school snack and how do you make it? The best answers make great reading.

### SQUARE OFF MAKES MATH FUN

Square Off is Prodigy's first on-line math game. You can play once a day, trying to beat your own high score and win recognition as the highest scorer of the week. The plot: With the help of SLAM5 (a superadvanced fifth-generation synthetic learning acceleration machine), your job is to solve math problems to defeat Opterm, a dangerous plot by the evil Colonel Blight and his DOG (Defense Obliteration Group). Each day, SLAM5 gives you a Wisdom Bit and comments on your work as you play.

# Calculate Your Weight on Other Planets

If your computer has DOS 5.0 or later, you can use the following QuickBASIC program to find out your weight on other planets.

Start by typing QBASIC at the DOS prompt. Type in the program lines below. If a line is indented, that means you should continue typing on the same line.

Note that a word followed by a colon is called a *subroutine*—a named branch of the program that's started, or *called,* from another branch. The GOTO command tells the program to go to the branch with that name. To find out more about other commands in this program, consult QuickBASIC help.

Once you've typed in all the lines and saved the program as WEIGHT.BAS, go to the Run menu and select Start. Then have fun!

Here's the program:

```
REM WEIGHT.BAS
REM Tells your weight on different
   planets.
CLS
INPUT "What's your name? ", userName$
PRINT
PRINT "Greetings, "; userName$; "! How
   many pounds do you weigh?"
INPUT WEIGHT%
CHOOSE:
PRINT
PRINT "Pick the number of the planet you
   want to weigh in on:"
PRINT
PRINT , "1. Mercury    6. Saturn"
PRINT , "2. Venus      7. Uranus"
PRINT , "3. Earth      8. Neptune"
PRINT , "4. Mars       9. Pluto"
PRINT , "5. Jupiter   10. The Moon"
PRINT
INPUT "Please select a number: ", Planet%
PRINT
SELECT CASE Planet%
```

```
CASE 1
PRINT "On Mercury, you'd weigh"; (WEIGHT%
   * .4); "pounds!"
CASE 2
PRINT "On Venus, you'd weigh"; (WEIGHT% *
   .9); "pounds!"
CASE 3
PRINT "On Earth, you weigh"; WEIGHT%;
   "pounds!"
CASE 4
PRINT "On Mars, you'd weigh"; (WEIGHT% *
   .4); "pounds!"
CASE 5
PRINT "On Jupiter, you'd weigh"; (WEIGHT%
   * 2.5); "pounds!"
CASE 6
PRINT "On Saturn, you'd weigh"; (WEIGHT%
   * .9); "pounds!"
CASE 7
PRINT "On Uranus, you'd weigh"; (WEIGHT%
   * .8); "pounds!"
CASE 8
PRINT "On Neptune, you'd weigh"; (WEIGHT%
   * 1.2); "pounds!"
CASE 9
PRINT "On Pluto, you'd weigh"; (WEIGHT% *
   .06); "pounds!"
CASE 10
PRINT "On the Moon, you'd weigh";
   (WEIGHT% * .17); "pounds!"
CASE ELSE
PRINT
PRINT "Please enter a number between 1
   and 10: "
PRINT
GOTO CHOOSE
END SELECT
PRINT
PRINT "Do you want to weigh in on another
   planet? (y/n)"
INPUT AGAIN$
AGAIN:
IF AGAIN$ = "y" THEN
GOTO CHOOSE
ELSEIF AGAIN$ = "n" THEN
GOTO BYE
ELSE
GOTO OOPS
END IF
OOPS:
PRINT
PRINT "Please enter y or n."
INPUT AGAIN$
GOTO AGAIN
BYE:
PRINT
PRINT "OK, "; userName$; ", thanks for
   playing!"
PRINT
SYSTEM
```

# Guess the Mystery Tune

The following program uses QuickBASIC's PLAY command to play a piece of music. Once you start QuickBASIC (see the "Calculate Your Weight on Other Planets" project), type in the MYSTERY.BAS file below and select Run, Start. Listen to the music and name that tune. (For the answer see the key at the back of this book.)

```
REM MYSTERY.BAS
REM Do you know the name of this song?
PLAY "L3G E C <G L8A B >C <L4A >L8C <L2G
  P4"
PLAY ">L3D G E C <L8A B >C L4D L8E L2D
  P8"
PLAY "L8E F E D L4G L8E D L3C P4"
PLAY "L8D L4C L8C <L4A >L8C <A L3G P4"
PLAY "L8G >L4C L8E L4D P8 C L8E D E F G
  E C L4D <L8G >L2C"
```

It's also easy to write your own tunes in QuickBASIC. Here are the rules.

- Unless you specify otherwise (look in QuickBASIC help for details), your tune will start in the fourth octave (which starts at middle C and goes up to B). Put the notes to be played in quotes after the PLAY command.

- Set the length of the notes by placing an L and a number before the notes to be played. L1 makes the following notes whole notes, L2 makes them half notes, L4 makes them quarter notes, and so on.

- Switch octaves by including the less-than sign (<) to go down an octave or the greater than sign (>) to go up an octave.

- You can specify rests, or pauses, by using P1 for a whole rest, P2 for a half rest, and so on.

# Change Your Prodigy Path

There are so many places to go on Prodigy, it helps to have a handy list of Jumpwords so you can get to your favorite places quickly. Prodigy lets you do this on line with the Path command. Once you've set up your path, you can hit **P** for Path and go to your favorite places automatically. When you first enroll in Prodigy, a Path is set up for you. To change it, follow this procedure.

1. Start by viewing your current Pathlist. To do this, select View Your Pathlist from the Jump menu. You can explore any of the places on the current Pathlist by double-clicking on the item.

2. To change the Pathlist, hit the Change Path button in the Pathlist window. Once you get to the Changepath screen, you'll see a numbered Pathlist with buttons to Add, Delete, Rearrange, or Goto any of the places on the list. Start by deleting any places you know you don't want on the list—hit the Delete button, and then type in the number of the item you want to remove. To add a new item, hit the Add button. Two buttons, labeled Previous Location and Other Location, will appear. Choose the Other Location button, type the Jumpword of the place you want to add, and specify where you want it to be on the list.

3. Try these Jumpwords and see if you like them enough to add to your Path:

| | |
|---|---|
| computer club | new |
| music charts | punchline |
| thinker | horoscope |
| politics | |

For a complete list of Jumpwords, select Index of Jumpwords from the Jump menu.

## You Be the Microprocessor (page 10)

Software Program 1: sugar cookies

Software Program 2: scrambled eggs

Software Program 3: pound cake

## Make a Pebble Computer (pages 10 and 11)

**1.**

1,492

747

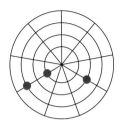

**2.**

$12 \times 3 = 36$

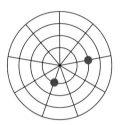

$231 + 445 = 676$

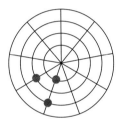

This multiplication is done by adding 12 together three times (12 + 12 + 12), which is exactly how an electronic computer does multiplication!

## Spell in Code (page 11)

1. Computers are cool.

Now I know my ABCs.

## How RAM Works (page 22)

A fool and his money are soon parted.

A penny saved is a penny earned.

Slow and steady wins the race.

Whoever dies with the most toys wins.

One man's ceiling is another man's floor.

A thing of beauty is a joy forever.

## You Be the Printer (page 22)

## Guess the Mystery Tune (page 49)

The tune is the first verse of the song "Daisy Bell," written and composed by Harry Dacre in 1892. It achieved some notoriety as the song that computer HAL 9000 sang in Stanley Kubrick's 1968 movie *2001: A Space Odyssey.*

Here are the lyrics:

Daisy, Daisy, give me your answer, do
I'm half crazy all for the love of you
It won't be a stylish marriage
I can't afford a carriage
But you'll look sweet
Upon the seat
Of a bicycle built for two.

The author and Ziff-Davis Press would like to thank the following people and companies for their contributions to this book.

## What Is a Computer?

### Pages 2 and 3

Cockpit: The Boeing Company
Psion Series 3 (hand-held PC): Psion, Inc.
Cray Supercomputer: Courtesy of Cray Research, Inc.

## Where Did Computers Come From?

### Pages 4 to 7

Charles Babbage and Difference Engine: Charles Babbage Institute, University of Minnesota
Stonehenge: William M. Roberts
Intel 4004 chip: Courtesy of Intel Corporation
Electron tube and transistor: AT&T Archives
Integrated circuit: Courtesy of National Semiconductor Corp.
ENIAC: School of Engineering and Applied Science, University of Pennsylvania

## The Rise of the Personal Computer

### Pages 8 and 9

Intel 8088, 80286, 80386, 80486, and both Pentium chips: Courtesy of Intel Corporation
Popular Electronics cover: Courtesy of Steve Mannes
Apple I, 1984 Apple Macintosh, and Macintosh SE: Courtesy of Apple Computer, Inc.
5¼-inch disk: Kenneth Rice Photography
Early hard disk: Seagate Technology
Bill Gates photograph: Courtesy of Microsoft Corp.
1981 IBM PC: Courtesy of International Business Machines Corporation
1983 Compaq Portable Computer: Reprinted with permission of Compaq Computer Corp. All Rights Reserved
Leading Edge Computer: Kenneth Rice Photography

## Inside a Computer Box

### Pages 14 and 15

Motherboard and power supply provided by Lightning Computers, Inc.
Computer box, motherboard, power supply, and ports: Kenneth Rice Photography

## Memory and Storage

### Pages 16 and 17

Memory chips provided by Lightning Computers, Inc.
Floppy disks, CD-ROM disk, and memory chips: Kenneth Rice Photography

## Input and Output

### Pages 18 and 19

Mouse and printer: Kenneth Rice Photography

## Printers

### Pages 20 and 21

William Hewlett and David Packard photograph: Courtesy of Hewlett-Packard Company
Baby: Jean Atelsek

## Binary Basics

### Pages 24 and 25

Samuel Morse photograph: Yale University Archives, Manuscript and Archives, Yale University Library
Digitized music provided by 3M Corporation

## DOS Basics

### Pages 26 to 29

MS-DOS package: Courtesy of Microsoft Corp.

## Programming

### Pages 40 and 41

Joseph-Marie Jacquard portrait: Board of Trustees of the Victoria & Albert Museum, London

## Programming Languages

### Pages 42 and 43

John Kemeny and Thomas Kurtz photograph: Dartmouth College Archives

## Games, Sound, and Graphics

### Pages 44 and 45

SimCity screen: Courtesy of Maxis
Where in Space Is Carmen Sandiego? screen: Courtesy of Broderbund
World Circuit screen: MicroProse® Software, Inc.
Super Sensory Chess game: Courtesy of Tandy Corporation/Radio Shack
Clip art and screen of Print Shop Deluxe: Courtesy of Broderbund

## Prodigy

### Pages 46 and 47

All screen images: ©1993 Prodigy Services Company

# EAST WOODS SCHOOL
31 Yellow Cote Road, Oyster Bay, New York 11771
Phone (516) 922-4400 Fax (516) 922-2589